Bhajanamritam

2018 Supplement

Mata Amritanandamayi Center
San Ramon, California, USA

Bhajanamritam Supplement 2018

Published By:
Mata Amritanandamayi Center
P.O. Box 613, San Ramon, CA 94583-0613
USA
www.amma.org

First printing by MA Center: May 2018

Address in India:
Mata Amritanandamayi Mission Trust
Amritapuri, Kollam Dt.
Kerala 690546, India
www.amritapuri.org
inform@amritapuri.org

Europe: www.amma-europe.org

About Pronunciation

The following key is for the guidance of those who are unfamiliar with the transliteration codes used in this book:

A	-as	a	in America
AI	-as	ai	in aisle
AU	-as	ow	in how
E	-as	e	in they
I	-as	ea	in heat
O	-as	o	in or
U	-as	u	in suit
KH	-as	kh	in Eckhart
G	-as	g	in give
GH	-as	gh	in loghouse
PH	-as	ph	in shepherd
BH	-as	bh	in clubhouse
TH	-as	th	in lighthouse
DH	-as	dh	in redhead
CH	-as	ch-h	in staunch-heart
JH	-as	dge	in hedgehog
Ñ	-as	ny	in canyon
Ṣ	-as	sh	in shine
Ś	-as	c	in efficient
Ṅ	-as	ng	in sing, (nasal sound)
V	-as	v	in valley
ZH	-as	rh	in rhythm
R	-as	r	in ride

Vowels with a line on top are pronounced like the vowels listed above but held twice as long.
The letters with dots under them (ṭ, ṭh, ḍ, ḍh, ṇ) are palatal sounds. They are pronounced with the tip of the tongue against the hard palate.

Table of Contents

Ādhyātmata (Kannada) 7
Ādiśaktī (Marathi) 8
Ādisivan (Tamil) 9
Ā... ē... ō... (Malayalam) 10
Aik manujā (Marāṭhi) 12
Amma ninna karagaḷalli (Kannada) 13
Anbumigu endan tāyē (Tamil) 14
Ārārum kāṇāte (Malayalam) 16
Ārupaṭai vīṭu (Tamil) 17
Āvo mā de caraṇā (Punjabi) 18
Āyī tujhē dāri (Maraṭhi) 20
Barpēr barpēr (Tulu) 21
Bhakti bhāvam (Telugu) 22
Bhāv phulānci (Marathi) 23
Bomma bomma (Hindi) 24
Calitam skhalitam (Malayalam) 25
Cinnāri ponnārī (Telugu) 26
Citta spandana (Kannada) 28
Cuṭalayil (Malayalam) 29
Darśanam darśanam sudarśanam (Telugu) 31
Ēlīlēlēlō (Malayalam) 32
Ennuṭe jīvita (Kannada version) 34
Entō tiraññu (Malayalam) 35
Ērēri ērēri (Malayalam) 36
Gajamukha pūjita (Telugu) 39
Gala gala (Telugu) 41
Hara hara śivanē (Tamil) 42

Hārati gaikonumā (Telugu) 43
Hariyuva nadiya (Gujarati version) 44
Har pal har kṣaṇ (Hindi) 45
Jag janani (Punjabi) 46
Jamunā ke taṭ par (Hindi) 47
Japonām japonām (Bengali) 49
Kāla bhairavā (Kannada) 50
Kālam kanalu (Tamil version) 51
Kala nuṇḍi kala loniki (Telugu) 52
Kānalēkunnānu ammā (Telugu) 54
Kaṇṇā kaṇṇā kaṇṇā (Tamil) 55
Kaṇṇā... un ninaivil (Tamil) 56
Karīndra vadanā (Hindi) 57
Kehendā hai mukh (Punjabi) 59
Ke rādhā mane tu (Gujarati) 60
Koṭānukoṭī (Gujarati version) 62
Koyi sūṇe nā sūṇe (Gujarati) 63
Kṛṣṇā karuṇadi kṛpe (Kannada) 64
Kūgi karedē (Kannada) 65
Mahāmahima (Kannada) 66
Manasā vācā (Marathi version) 67
Mayil pīlī (Malayalam) 68
Nā guṇḍe (Telugu) 69
Nāṭakam onṭru (Tamil) 70
Nīlāmbuja nayane (Gujarati version) 71
Nīlāmbuja nayane (Tamil version) 72
Nirmala jīvana (Kannada) 72
Oṭa kuzhalūti (Malayalam) 73
Paritiyinmun paniyai (Tamil) 74

Paurṇṇamirāvil (Kannada version) 75
Paurṇṇamirāvil (Telugu) 76
Prati lēdu (Telugu) 77
Rādhārāṇī ke pyāre (Hindi) 78
Rām nām ras (Hindi) 79
Samsāraduḥkha (Telugu version) 81
Śankaranandana (Hindi) 82
Śaraṇennirō (Kannada) 83
Seyda seyalgaḷ (Tamil) 84
Śrī laḷitāmbikē sarvaśakte (Kannada version) 86
Śyām-golok-me (Hindi) 88
Tannanna tannanna (Malayalam) 89
Tāttinantam teytārā (Malayalam) 93
Tintinnam tintinnam (Malayalam) 95
Tum ho māte (Hindi) 97
Undan tōḷil (Tamil) 98
Vandē vēdamayīm (Sanskrit) 99
Vicalita vāgade (Kannada) 100
Viṭhal smaraṇ karā 101
Yād rakh bande (Hindi) 103
Yād teri vic (Punjabi) 104
Yaśodānā lāl (Gujarati) 105

Ādhyātmata (Kannada)

ādhyātmata anantāgasata munte
tantu nilisite nanna ō tante
ādarāgadalla ī puṭṭa hakkige
ākāśadalli rekke biccalu
sūryaneḍege lagge hākalu

O Lord, You have brought me in front of the limitless sky of spirituality. I am but a small fledgling, I cannot spread my wings in the sky nor fly towards the sun.

huṭṭinontigide ī kalbaṇṭe dēvi
puṭṭa hakkiya koraḷalli bhārā
prārabdha bhāra jaggutiralintu
svacchanda bānāṭi hēgāgali?
sūryaneḍege lagge hākali?

Right from the time of my birth, a huge rock of prarabdha has been tied to my little feet, burdening me. How can I become a free bird, how can I fly towards the sun?

sūryaneḍege lagge hākuvē – āka
sūryaneḍege lagge hākkuvē – nā
sūryaneḍege lagge hākuvē
sūryaneḍege lagge hākuvē

I will surely fly towards the sun.

puṭṭadontu hejje nā iṭaballenammā
uḷita ombattu ninnadāgatē?
ettaradintali bīḷadantiralu ettikō
ninnettarakkenna parāśakti
ninnettarakkenna parāśakti

I will take one baby step, Mother, won't You take the nine remaining steps? Please hold me so that I don't fall down, please hold me close to You, O Parashakti.

Ādiśaktī (Marathi)

ādiśaktī āyī bhavānī
he ambe śaktidāyinī, bhaktidāyinī
premadāyinī, viśvās dāyinī
ādimāye jagatkāriṇī
he ambe śaktidāyinī, bhaktidāyinī
premadāyinī, viśvās dāyinī

Primal energy, Mother Bhavani, O Mother, giver of energy, devotion, love and faith! You create the illusory world, O Mother, and give energy, devotion, love and faith!

ajāṇa lekare tujhī āmhi
vyākuḷ jhālo yā samsārī
śaraṇ ālo tav caraṇī
śaktidāyinī, bhaktidāyinī
premadāyinī, viśvās dāyinī

Sorrowful and ignorant, we now seek refuge at Your feet, O Mother. You are the giver of energy, devotion, love and faith.

māgato tuj āmhī... śakti de jagadambe
māgato tuj āmhī... bhakti de jagadambe
māgato tuj āmhī... prem de jagadambe
māgato tuj āmhī... viśvās devūn
rakṣaṇ kar jagadambe

Today we beg of You... give us strength O Mother of all! Today we beg of You... give us devotion, O Mother of all! Today we beg of You, give us love and faith O Mother of all!

Ādisivan (Tamil)

ādisivan tōḷamarntu ātupāmbē - manam
ānavattāl ātum kūttai pāṭupāmbē
vēdamōtum tattuvattai kēḷupāmbē - manam
vēruvazhi ōtuvatēn kūrupāmbē

O Serpent who dances on Lord Shiva's shoulders, please narrate the drama of the mind that dances with the ego. Listen to the teachings of the Vedas. Tell us, why does the mind get distracted and run?

uṭamaiyilē ānavattāl ātukirārē - ellām
uṭayavanin uṭamaiyanṭrō kūrupāmbē
uravinilē ānavattāl ātukirārē - uyir
uṭalai viṭṭāl uravumuṇḍō kūrupāmbē

People are egoistic about their possessions. Doesn't everything indeed belong to the Lord? People are egoistic about their relationships. Do relationships have any existence once life leaves the body?

bhaktiyilē ānavattāl ātukirārē - ōṭṭai
pānaiyatu niraintiṭumō kūrupāmbē
jñānattilē ānavattāl ātukirārē - nañcu
kalantapinnē viruntumuṇḍō kūrupāmbē

People are egoistic about their devotion. Does a pot with a hole ever become full? People are egoistic about their knowledge. Can there be a feast once poison is mixed in the food?

hara hara hara hara hara - ena haranai nāṭuvōm
śiva śiva śiva śiva ena solli śiva padam aṭaivōm

Let us seek refuge by calling out to Hara. Let us reach His feet by calling out to Shiva!

Ā... ē... ō... (Malayalam)

ā... ē... ō...
ā... ē... ō...
attinantam tintaka tārā
tinantinantam tintaka tārā
teytārā teytārā tintaka tāraka tārō
teytārā teytārā tintaka tintaka tārō
teytārā teytārā tintaka tintaka tārō

Joy and happiness abound! Listen to the rhythm of the drums!

tāḷattil cuvaṭu veccē cuvaṭatinottini
meyyumuzhiññē
kāśipurādhīśanavan ini narttanamāṭu hṛttil
kāśipurādhīśanavan ini narttanamāṭu hṛttil

Swaying to the rhythmic beats, O Lord Shiva, God of Kashi (Varanasi), please dance within my heart!

ceñciṭayil gangayoḷiccē gangayoṭottaṇiyambiḷikkīr
kāśipurādhīśanavan ini narttanamāṭu hṛttil
kāśipurādhīśanavan ini narttanamāṭu hṛttil

With the holy Ganges hiding in Your matted hair, and the crescent moon shining on top, O Lord Shiva, God of Kashi, please dance within my heart!

veṇṇīrāl mēnimimukki mēniyilāke pāmbu puḷaññē
kāśipurādhīśanavan ini narttanamāṭu hṛttil
kāśipurādhīśanavan ini narttanamāṭu hṛttil

With holy ash smeared all over Your body, adorned by slithering snakes... O Lord Shiva, God of Kashi, please dance within my heart!

ānattōl meniputaccē mēniyilāyoru villumaṇiññē
kāśipurādhiśanavan ini narttanamāṭu hṛttil
kāśipurādhiśanavan ini narttanamāṭu hṛttil

With an elephant hide to clothe your body, holding a bow in Your hands, O Lord Shiva, God of Kashi, please dance within my heart!

nantuṇitan tāḷamuraññē tāḷamuraññatu mēḷamiyannē
kāśipurādhiśanavan ini narttanamāṭu hṛttil
kāśipurādhiśanavan ini narttanamāṭu hṛttil

As the beats of the nantuni (musical instrument) become stronger and faster, O Lord Shiva, God of Kashi, please dance within my heart!

mukkaṇṇil tīyumericcu tīyatilonnāyi tṛpuramericcu
kāśipurādhiśanavan ini narttanamāṭu hṛttil
kāśipurādhiśanavan ini narttanamāṭu hṛttil

With fire kindled from his third eye, He destroyed Tripura, the three worlds where demons lived. O Lord Shiva, God of Kashi, please dance within my heart!

gaurīśā tiruvaṭiyē tiruvaṭivārnnoru nānmaraye
kāśipurādhiśanavan ini narttanamāṭu hṛttil
kāśipurādhiśanavan ini narttanamāṭu hṛttil

O Lord of Gauri, You are the physical embodiment of the four Vedas. O Lord Shiva, God of Kashi, please dance within my heart!

Aik manujā (Marāṭhi)

aik manujā tulā miḷāli hī durlabha narakāyā
dharuni viṣayāncā sanga nakō ghālavū hī vāyā
dēvānē dilī hī kāyā āpulēci svarūp ōḷakhāyā
guru māūlīcā upadeś ghēī satvar bhavanadī utarāyā

O Man, listen! You have obtained this human birth which is difficult to attain. Do not waste it by clinging to the senses. The Almighty has given you this body so that you may realize your true nature. Hearken to the teaching of the Guru-Mother: that the river of samsara (cycle of births and deaths) has hidden your true nature.

sōdōniyā viṣayāñci gōḍī ghēūni tava antarangi buḍī
lāvī satsangāci gōḍī yēṇē tū viṣayānanda tōḍī
rāhūni sāvadhān harghaḍī dēkhijē manācyā tū uḍī
āḷavī pāṇḍuranga āvaḍī tēṇē lāgēla brahmarasācī gōḍī

Detach yourself from sense pleasures. Dive deep into your inner self. Relish satsang (the company of the holy) and thus renounce sense pleasures. Remain awake and alert at all times and thereby witness the mind's distractions. Always revere Pāṇḍuranga (a manifestation of Lord Vişhṇu), and come to realize the essence of Brahman, the Supreme.

bhajare manujā pāṇḍuranga
jay hari viṭṭhalā pāṇḍuranga

O Man, contemplate the glories of Pāṇḍuranga! Victory to Lord Vitthala!

gurupadī śaraṇ jāūn dē manālā bhaktīcā ranga
bhavatāraka gurudēv karatīla jīvadaśā ajñānācā bhanga
bodhabhānu uday pāūnī prakaṭēl antarī pāṇḍuranga
janma maraṇācā cukēla fērā hōīl jīvan abhanga

Surrender at the Guru's feet. Immerse the mind in the colors of devotion. The spiritual master saves us from samsāra by destroying our ignorance of the Self. When the sun of wisdom dawns, Pāṇḍuranga manifests within us, bringing an end to the cycle of births and deaths, helping us realize the soul in its fullness.

Amma ninna karagaḷalli (Kannada)

amma ninna karagaḷalli kanda nānu
ninna prēmakkē ōḍōḍi bande nānu
amma nī kṛpe tōreyā
amma nī kṛpe tōreyā

O Mother, I am a child in Your arms. I ran to You to bask in Your love. Please shower Your grace on me!

dūrāseya sereyinda nannanu biḍisu
ari ṣaḍvargadinda enna mukti goḷisu
dveṣa svārtthagaḷinda nanna muktanāgisu
sad buddhiya koṭṭu śaraṇāgati nīḍu

Liberate me from hundreds of desires and from the six-fold enemy (lust, anger, delusion, greed, pride and jealousy). Free me from the grip of hatred and selfishness. Bestow intelligence on me and bless me with an attitude of surrender.

amma nī kṛpe tōreyā
amma nī kṛpe tōreyā

Please shower Your grace on me!

jaganmāteya arivukoṭṭu samśaya tolagisu
ellarallu ninnane kāṇuva dṛṣṭi nīḍu
samsāra bandhadinda nannanu biḍisu
mōkṣava nīḍi nammanu harasu

Bestow on me the knowledge that You are Mother of the Universe. Dispel my doubts, help me see You in all. Free me from the clutches of samsāra (cycle of life and death), and grant me Liberation.

Anbumigu endan tāyē (Tamil)

anbumigu endan tāyē
ādarippāy enḍrum nīyē
aruḷamudai anaittilum pozhindu
allalkaḷai kaḷaindiḍuvāyē

O loving Mother of mine, protect us always. Shower Your grace on all, thereby keeping at bay all suffering.

enkaḷ uḷḷam unayē ninaindu
ēttramura nalvazhi kāṭṭu
uyirkaḷellām un vaḍivena nānkaḷ
uṇarndiḍa madimayakkam nīkku

May our minds dwell on You always. Show us the right path. Awaken the understanding that all beings are Your diverse forms, and thus dispel our ignorance.

nittiyamē! nirmalamē! teḷḷamudē! tīñcuvayē!

O Eternal One, Immaculate One! You are full of nectar, the very essence of sweetness!

uttam suttrum ūrum pērum
sottu sukham pattrukaḷ palavum
viṭṭakala vinaikaḷ kaḷaivāy
viraindemmai malaraḍi sērppāy

Forsaking family and friends, name and fame, wealth and pleasures, may we quickly become One with Your holy feet.

nittam nī em ninaivinil ninḍru
nittiya porpadankaḷai padittu
sattiya tattuva pada nizhalil
śaraṇāgata nargati aruḷvāy

May we always harbor thoughts of You. May Your footprints impress themselves in our hearts. Bless us so that we may take refuge in the shade of Truth.

Ārārum kāṇāte (Malayalam)

ārārum kāṇāte ārārum kēḷkkāte
karayukayāyirunnennum – karaḷviṅgi
karayukayāyirunnennum
karuṇatan niravē, nin ninavennil kuḷiriḷam
himarēṇudhāra pōlutirū – atilōla
hṛdayattil puḷakaccārttaṇiyū

Unseen, and unheard, I was crying everyday from deep within my heart. O abundance of compassion, Your memories are flowing in me like a constant stream of water cascading from the mountains. Please come to my aching heart and bestow happiness.

arimullappū-viṭarttīṭuvān-ettumī
ariya-nilāvilūṭaṇayū – sarasamī
saraḷa-nilāvilūṭaṇayū
karaḷin kiṭārattil urukunna duḥkhattin
lāvāpravāhamī mizhinīr – aṇayātta
lāvāpravāhamī mizhinīr

Have You come as the shining moon who causes the jasmine buds to bloom at night? My tears are like flowing lava springing from deep inside my heart where my sorrows melt.

oru-tiri-mizhiveṭṭam oru-tari kāruṇyam
coriyān-itentēyamāntam – hṛdayattil
utirān-itentēyamāntam
janimṛtikk-uttaram tēṭunna yōgikaḷkk-
ātmānubhūti tan lahari – aviṭunnu
amṛtānubhūti tan lahari

Why is it taking You so long to grace me with Your glance, or even shower me with a little compassion? Why so long in coming to my heart? The sages who search for answers for birth and death experience Your intoxicating presence. You are the intoxicating experience of immortal bliss.

Ārupaṭai vīṭu (Tamil)

ārupaṭai vīṭu koṇḍa murugā murugā
ānaimugan sōdaranē murugā murugā
ādiśivan jñānamuṭan
annaiyavaḷ śaktiyuṭan
ārumuganāga vanda tirumāl marugā

O Lord Muruga, You have six sacred houses (temples), and are the brother of the elephant-faced Ganesha. You came with Supreme knowledge. Shakti is Your mother, and You have six faces!

vēṇḍāda ānavattāl vizhalāy ānayendan
vidhiyai māttriṭuvāy vēlmurugā
māṇḍālum unnaṭiyai maravādirukkumoru
manamadai tandiṭuvāy mālmarugā
manamadai tandiṭuvāy
murugā... murugā... murugā...

O Muruga, please change my destiny that has become a quagmire due to my unwanted ego. Give me a mind that never forgets You even at the time of death.

āṇḍāṇḍu kālamendan arivai maraittukkoṇḍu
āsai vaḷargiradē vēlmurugā
pūṇḍōṭu adai azhittu pudiya piravi tandu
pudumaṇam vīsacceyvāy mālmarugā
pudumaṇam vīsacceyvāy
murugā... murugā... murugā...

With the passing years, my desires are increasing and clouding my mind. Please uproot these desires, give me a new birth and let me spread a new fragrance.

vēlmurugā harōharā...
mālmarugā harōharā
kandanukku harōharā
kaṭambanukku harōharā
muruganukku harōharā
kumaranukku harōharā
kandanukku kaṭambanukku
muruganukku kumarunukku
harōharā, harōharā, haraharōharā

Āvo mā de caraṇā (Punjabi)

āvo mā de caraṇā vicc sir nivāyiye
gajvaj ke mā di fateh bulāyiye

Come rest your head at the holy feet of the Mother. Sing and rejoice, calling 'Victory to Mother!'

terī ik nazar ne mayyā
premjyot hai jalāyi
puleyā is duniyā nu
dendī tū dikhāyī

One glance from You, O Mother, has lit the flame of love. Calling the world, You have revealed Your Self.

jap jap terā nām mayyā amṛt pīvā
bas tūhī hūṇ mayyā jag ho gayā phikkā
sirjan hār tū hī kaṇ kaṇ vicc tū hī
jag upjeyā tere tom me ram jāṇā
ram jāṇā ram jāṇā hai

We chant again and again the immortal nectar of Your name. You are the only One, O Mother, all is meaningless without You. Supreme protector, You reside in every particle. O Creator, it is through You that I have come to the Lord.

hasdā peyā rovā jag kahe kamlā
tū hī das mā me kamlā yā jag kamlā
sirjan hār tū hī kaṇ kaṇ vich tū hī
jag upjeyā tere tom me ram jāṇā
ram jāṇā ram jāṇā hai

Seeing my laughing and crying, the world calls me mad. Tell me Mother, is it me or the world that is mad? Supreme protector, You reside in every particle. O Creator, it is through You that I have come to the Lord.

jay jay jay mā... jay mā... jay mā... pukār
jay jay jay mā... jay mā... jay mā... pukār
jay jay jay mā... jay mā... jay mā... pukār
jay jay jay mā... jay mā... jay mā... pukār

Victory to the Mother, call out 'Victory to the Mother!'

Āyī tujhē dāri (Maraṭhi)

āyī tujhē dāri aj jōgavā māgate
tujhī bhakti karitā aj jōgavā māgate
māye jogavā de māye jogavā de
dega ādi māye bhavānī jogavā maj de

O Mother, I stand at Your door asking for alms. Your bhakti alone I shall take as alms. Mother give me alms, O Mother give me alms. Primordial One, Mother of Illusion, Bhavani, please give me alms today.

tujhī kṛpādṛṣṭīj māye pānguḷ kari gaman
tujhī kṛpāśaktīj māye mūkh hoyī vācak
bhaktīrasāt tujhīyā gunthūn jāvo jogavā de
sakaḷ janm-maraṇācā pherā miṭe jogavā de

Your glance of grace alone can make the lame walk. The strength of Your grace can make the dumb talk. O Mother, let me forget myself in devotion to You alone. Give me alms, that the cycle of births and deaths may come to an end.

māye jogavā de māye jogavā de
dega ādi māye bhavāni jogavā maj de

O Mother give me alms, give me alms. Primordial One, Mother of Illusion, Bhavani, please give me alms today.

anant sevā caraṇī tujhe lābh jogavā de
nāhī kāhī bodh pūrṇ-bodh jogavā de
manovikār sāṇḍūn tujhe vicār jogavā de
nisang ho māye itun sang tujhe jogavā de

Give me alms of having the opportunity to do seva at Your feet. Give me alms of total awareness, O Mother, because I have no awareness at all. Give me alms of Your thoughts alone so that I can get be rid of all unwanted thoughts. Give me alms of ever being in association with You, that I may become dissociated from maya (illusion).

Barpēr barpēr (Tulu)

barpēr barpēr namma ammā barpēr
bāle manasa da śuddha bhaktig ō konvēr
ajñāna kaḷeyuna sujñāna boḷpād
bhakti bhāvōda leppug taḍa malpande barpēr

If we call out to Mother with innocent devotion, She will hear our call. She will come as the light of knowledge to dispel the darkness of ignorance. When we call with innocent devotion, the Goddess comes at once.

bāḷvēda lakṣyōn teripāyare bhūmig jatter
ā durgā paramēśvarī ammanē olid batter
sādi tōjante bult leppunaga ammanē
kain patud naḍapāvera appe karuṇēḍē

Mother incarnated on earth to show us the purpose of a human life. Goddess Durga came in response to our call. If we call out to Mother when we are lost, She will compassionately lead us by the hand.

leppugā ammanē leppugā ō ammā balē ammā

Let us call out 'O Mother! Please come, Mother!'

tappuleg kṣame kordu eḍḍe sādi tōjāver
pāpa kaḷed kāpvērammā śaraṇāgata bhakterena
nisvārttha sēve malpi bhaktereg varadāyini
nirmala manasa da cittōḍ telita nalipverammā

Mother forgives us our mistakes and shows us the noble path. She rids devotees who have taken refuge in Her of their sins. Mother is a boon-bestowing Goddess to devotees who do selfless service. She dances blissfully in a pure mind.

Bhakti bhāvam (Telugu)

bhakti bhāvameppuḍu vastundō?
nākā bhakti bhāvameppuḍu vastundō?
nī pēru talaci kannīru kārce rōju
eppuḍu vastundō? ārōjeppuḍu vastundō?

O Mother, when will I be blessed with that exalted mood of devotion towards You? When shall I attain that state of devotional ecstasy? When shall tears flow from my eyes upon the mere uttering of Your name? When will that day come? O Mother...

paramahamsa amma kai
tapincina vēdana
rādhamma kṛṣṇuni kai
cintincina tapana
amma... amma... amma... amma...

When will I experience the pain of separation from the Divine Mother that was undergone by Sri Ramakrishna Paramahamsa? When will I experience the agony of longing for Lord Krishna that was suffered by Mother Radha? O Mother.

ānjanēyuḍi rāmanāma japa kīrttana
prahlāduni sarvatra hari darśana
amma... amma... amma... amma...

When will I experience the ecstasy of Hanuman upon chanting Sri Rama's holy name? When will I be blessed with Prahalad's vision of seeing Lord Vishnu everywhere? O Mother...

Bhāv phulānci (Marathi)

bhāv phulānci phulānci māḷā
arppin māzyā, māzyā ambā mātela

I offer a flower garland of my emotions to my Mother Amba.

hṛday mandīri ambā bhagavati
jīv jaḍalā ticyā vartti
joḍoniya kar śrīcarṇāla
arppin māzyā, māzyā ambā mātela
naman ādiśakti devi bhavatāriṇi bhayahāriṇi
bhāv phulānci

In the temple of my heart is Mother Bhagavati. Bowing to Her auspicious feet, I give my life to Her. Prostrations to You, primal energy! You take us across the ocean of transmigration, You destroy fear.

bhakticā hā dhāgā ghevūni
premāci tī phule vecūni
ḍoḷe bharūn pāhīn ambela
arpin māzyā, māzyā ambā mātela
naman ādiśakti devi bhavatāriṇi bhayahāriṇi
bhāv phulānci

Taking this thread of devotion, stringing it with the flowers of love, I rejoice with the vision of Mother... Prostrations to You, primal energy! You take us across the ocean of transmigration, You destroy fear.

ajñānāci karunī vāt
jñānāci tī lāvūn jot
ātmasvarūpi miḷvīn ambela
arpin māzyā, māzyā ambā mātela
naman ādiśakti devi bhavatāriṇi bhayahāriṇi
bhāv phulānci

Our Mother Amba, makes us become One with our true Self by destroying ignorance and lighting the lamp of Knowledge. Prostrations to You, primal energy! You take us across the ocean of transmigration, You destroy fear.

Bomma bomma (Hindi)

This is a traditional song composed of drum beats and devotional sounds signifying joy and happiness, as an homage to Ganesh. Therefore there is no translation.

bomma bomma tā thaiyya thaiyya nakk
dinākk nakku din bhajan kare
udanitanāk dhimi titām titām tom
thai thai gaṇapati nām sadā

dhimmi kiṭukiṭa dhimmi kiṭukiṭa
dikktāḷa dhimmikkiṭu
takiṭa takiṭa taḷa tavoṭutām
udanitanāk dhimi titām titām tōm
thai thai gaṇapati nām sadā

avaru bāsukai karambhājiti
akenām catur gaṇarājā
tāḷamandira bahut dāmsat
suramaṇḍalakī surabājā

veṇuvāsare amṛtakuṇḍaliki
tārikirikiṭa tārikirikiṭa tavālgajā
nārada tumburu vaiṇavajāhe
nārada gaṇame uvasarjā

avaru bāsukai karambhājiti
dhṛmidhṛmi dhṛmidhṛmi mirutankā
navāp sārangi sitāri kiṇari
avaru bāsukai mukharsingā

Calitam skhalitam (Malayalam)

calitam skhalitam mama manamammē
prākṛta prakṛtam mama manaḥ
viphala vilāpam vikala vicāram
mama mānasa sahacārikaḷāy

O Mother, my mind is wavering and wild by nature. Fruitless wailing and dark thoughts are cohabitants in my mind.

avikala buddhiyaruḷukayammē
sakala-kalāmayi saraḷatayēkū
sattva-rajas-tama guṇabhēdaṅgaḷ
cittākāśē ceyvū vihāram
kāḷi kapālini kayyil-eṭukkū
vāḷum śūlavum samhārārttham
ahamkṛtiyākum dārikadaityan
ghōraparākrami viharati manasi

O Mother please bestow an intellect that sees oneness in everything. Embodiment of all arts, please bless me with simplicity. May the three gunas (qualities) reside in the sky of my mind. O Kali, please take the sword and trident in hand for destruction. The demon Darika (that is my ego) resides in my mind as a ferocious warrior.

maṭiyarutammē vaikarut-iniyum
vīzhttarut-ivane bhavāmbudhitannil
bhīmākāram pūṇḍatha munnil
janmāntara kṛta-duṣkarmmaṅgaḷ
vanniṭu munnil varadē dēvī
kaitavanāśini kāḷi mahēśi
citta-viśuddhiyum bhōga-vimuktiyum
jīvan muktiyum-ekūka caṇḍī

Mother! Do not hesitate or delay any longer. Do not let me fall into the ocean of transmigration (the cycle of birth and death). All bad deeds from previous lives have assumed the colossal form of Bhima. Please appear before me, Divine Mother, bestower of boons. Kali Maheshi, destroyer of sorrow, O Chandi! Please bestow on me purity of mind, free me from materialism, and grant me ultimate liberation.

Cinnāri ponnārī (Telugu)

cinnāri ponnārī kṛṣṇayyā
nīvu ekkaḍa unnāvayyā
ēkamai gokulamu
vediki alisenayyā

O darling little Krishna, where are You? I have become weary, having searched all of Gokul for You...

āturatō yaśōdammā
vākililō vēcēnu
lōgililō gōpammalū
vēcēnu ninnu bandhimpagā

Mother Yashoda is eagerly waiting for You at the door. The gopis are waiting on the verandah to bind You with their love.

jābillī mōmu cūḍagā
rādhārāṇi vecenu
punnamī vennala rātirilo
rāsalīla āḍuṭaku

Seeing Your face in the full moon, Radha-Rani comes to dance the rasalila with You.

veciyunnārū andaru
vetukutunnāru ellaru
cikkakuṇḍā nallanayyā
līlajesī āṭalāḍe

O Krishna! All are eagerly waiting for You, yet You remain elusive.

rāvayyā nallanayyā mudamunu nimpavayyā
cinnāri kṛṣṇayyā ponnārī kannayyā

O Krishna, please come! Darling little Krishna, fill us with divine love!

Citta spandana (Kannada)

citta spandana bhrameyīm manavanu tāyē
ātmānusandhāna deḍege harisu
kālanu anukṣaṇavū bennu hattiha
ō kāḷi karuṇeyīm nōḍu
ammā... ammā... ammā... ammā...

O Mother Divine! Please remove the mental confusion caused by the movements of the mind and tune my mind towards atma anusandhana (contemplation of my true Self). As moments pass by, Kala (the lord of death) is behind me. O Mother Kali with compassion filled eyes, look at me and see my plight. O Mother...

jīvanada yātreyali mōhāndhakāradali
muḷuki duḥkhavanuṇḍu manavu baḷali
dārikāṇade ninna baḷigē bandenu
kāḷi ninnāsareyu manada śamavu
ammā... ammā... ammā... ammā...

On this journey of life my mind became immersed in the darkness of attachments and is in great agony. Not knowing the way out from this, O Mother, I have come to You. Kali, refuge in You is the only total solace for this agitated mind of mine. O Mother...

bēḍanā baleyalli sikka jinkeya teradi
jīviyu māyeyali siluki baḷali
rakṣisu emmannu padakamaladaḍi
amaratvavanu emage nīḍu
ammā... ammā... ammā... ammā...

As a deer caught in the net of a hunter, similar is the plight of the individual caught in the snares of Maya. Protect me, O Mother, as I have taken refuge at Your lotus feet. Please bestow the knowledge of the Self, O Mother...

vivēka vairāgya emage nī nīḍammā
jñāna jyōtiya beḷagu hṛnmanadalī
ātmānusandhāna advaita bōdhisi
niratiśayānanda nīḍu
ammā... ammā... ammā... ammā...

Mother please give me discrimination and dispassion, please light the lamp of wisdom in my heart. Teach me the path of atma-anusandhana (contemplation of the Self) which leads to the ultimate goal of non-duality. Give me ever-new joy, O Mother.

Cuṭalayil (Malayalam)

cuṭalayil eriyum śarīram
pacca virakinu samamatu tanne
pērum perumayum-ārnna śarīram
pāzhil-eriññaṅgaṭaṅgum
tēṭuka tēṭuka martyā innu
tīyileriyātta ninnē...

Bodies burn in the funeral pyre. The body that once had name and fame is no different than the wood that is burning - it will be burned up. O Man, enquire today, search for the 'you' that cannot be burnt by fire!

ettippiṭiccum kuticcum - pinne
veṭṭippiṭiccum nī nēṭum
vittattin-entuṇḍiṅgarttham - ninde
pērum perumayum vyarttham...
innaleyennilla innilla pinne
nīrppōḷa pōle nī māyum
tēṭuka tēṭuka marttyā - ennum
nityamāyuḷḷoru ninnē

What is the meaning of the fortune that you have gained through so many ways? Your name and fame are worthless. You neither have yesterday nor today. You will simply fade away like a bubble in water. O Man, enquire today, search for the 'you' that is eternal!

pōratu nēṭuvānāyi - nīyō
pōrkkaḷamākkunnituḷḷam
anyane vennunī nēṭum - onnum
āvilla koṇḍaṅgu pōkān
entokke nēṭi nīyennāl - kaṭam
koṇḍatu pōlanī taḷḷum
tēṭuka tēṭuka marttyā - ennum
tannuṭētāyuḷḷa ninnē

By trying to win the war, you are creating a battlefield within yourself. You cannot take with you anything that you have gained in victory over others. You will need to leave behind everything that you have gained in this life. O Man, enquire today, search for the 'you' that is eternally your own.

Darśanam darśanam sudarśanam

(Telugu)

darśanam darśanam sudarśanam nityam
viśvarūpa samdarśanam
darśanam darśanam samdarśanam sudarśanam
nityadarśanam sarvadarśanam

Divine vision, awe-inspiring vision, the eternal vision of God's cosmic form. Divine vision, enthralling and complete vision, perpetual vision, Universal vision.

anēkamēkamugā manō samdarśanam
ā jagannāthunidarśanam
viśvanāthunigā viśvadarśanam
jñāna nētramula nityavīkṣaṇam
advaita-darśanam samdarśanam

It is a vision of seeing the many as One. It is a glimpse of the Lord of the Universe. It is an insight of looking at the creation as Creator. It is a perpetual awareness possessed by the seers of wisdom. It is the knowledge of oneness and the vision of eternal truth.

sahasra-nētramulu sahasra-vadanamulu
sahasra-karamulatō darśanam
sahasra pādamulaku-vandanam
sahasra-sūryula divyatējamu
sahasra-rūpa cit darśanam

A vision of thousands of eyes, thousands of faces, thousands of hands as One. It is a worship of thousands of feet, the brilliance of thousands of suns. It is an everlasting revelation of seeing the thousands of forms as a single universal consciousness.

namō vāsudēva... namō viśvanātha
namō jaganmāta... namō parabrahma

Salutations to Lord Vishnu who resides in every heart. Salutations to Shiva, the lord of Universe. Salutations to Parashakti, embodiment of cosmic energy. Salutations to Parabrahma, the ultimate reality.

Ēlīlēlēlō (Malayalam)

ēlīlēlēlō... taka ēlīlēlēlō
ēlīlēlēlō... taka ēlīlēlēlō
ēlīlēlō ēlīlēlō ēlīlēlēlō
ēlīlēlō ēlīlēlō ēlīlēlēlō

Joy and happiness abound!

cērttīṭānuḷḷil ennum rāmapādaṅgaḷ
ōrttupāṭānāy ennum rāmapādaṅgaḷ
nāḷitērē kāttirunnē tāpasi śabari
rāmapādam ōrttirunnē tāpasi śabari

Always keeping Lord Rama's feet in her heart, remembering and praising His feet, Saint Shabari waited a long time thinking only of Lord Rama's feet.

pāṭukillivịṭe oru kāṭṭupūpōlum
yogivaryanmār tavamārnna maṇṇitilāy
nāḷiteṇṇi kāttirunnē tāpasi śabari
rāmapādam kāttirunnē tāpasi śabari

Where great sages practice austerities and not even a wildflower is seen, Shabari waited for a long time, dwelling only on Lord Rama's feet.

rāvu māyukayāy bhuvi rāmananayukayāy
śrīpadaṅgaḷatā mizhiyārnnapuṇyamatāy
ādyavarṣa nīrmaṇipōl vīṇavaḷmunnil
ātmaharṣatīrtthamāyi śrīpadaṅgaḷārnnē

The night will end, Lord Rama will come, great visions and deeds will occur. Like the first drops of rain, she sang, her tears of joy washing His feet.

pērttukālamatāy hṛdiyōrttaneramatē
jīvapuṇyamatāy janiyārnnavāzhvatinē
kāttilāṭum ālilapōl kūppininnē munnil
ā kāraṅgaḷ cērttu māril ānayiccē pinnē

Then the longed-for, crowning moment arrived... and with hands shivering like banyan leaves, she welcomed the Lord into her heart.

pūvumānasamāy hṛdi dīpanāḷamatāy
tīrtthamāyatumē tiru rāmanāmamatē
ārnnavaḷā pūjakaḷum ācaraṇapuṇyam
pūjayārnnamānasaṅgaḷ īśvara vihāram

His holy name had become the light, His name had become the water that flowed from her core. In worship and ritual, her mind was fully given to God.

kāṭṭukāykaḷitā pinne pērttukaikaḷilāy
pākamonnariyān avaḷ kāṇitinnavayē
nīṭṭi pinne rāghavanāy ā kanikaḷ nērē
rāmanappōḷ prītiyōṭe ā pazhaṅgaḷ tinnē

The fruit that she plucked and tasted to make sure that it was sweet, She offered and He ate with pleasure! Her life was now complete.

pākamārnnuyirē bhaktiyōṭu nalkiṭukil
kāzhcayāyiṭumē atu īśanēttiṭumē
pāṭu pāṭu rāmanāmam mōkṣamēkum mantram
cērttuvakkyū vāzhvatilāy rāmanāmapuṇyam

When we offer our true devotion, God always receives us with pleasure. Let us sing Ram's liberating name, and always keep God's name close.

Ennuṭe jīvita (Kannada version)

en jīvita-naukeyu bhavasāgaratali
muḷugutalide ammā nōḍu

māyeya birukāḷi balavāgi bīsi
allōla kallōla enna suttā
manavemba cukkāṇi kaitappi ammā
baḷaluta liruve nānittā

aru vikāra rakkasi yarillī
hākuta liruvaru dōṇi huṭṭā
kāruṇyahīna birukāḷiyalī
dōṇiyō ākidē enna caṭṭā

jīvita naukeya bhakti cukkāṇi
chidrachidra vāgi bidditallā
viśvāsavemba hāyi ayyō
haridu cinti āyitallā

dōṇi taḷadi ontu randhravāgi
nīrō nīru dōṇi tumbā
nānēnu māḍali īgēnu māḍali
tiḷisikoḍu bā ammā

āvarisi kattale ettettalū
nānata roḷage silukiruvē
muḷuguva munna ninnane nambi
'ammā, nannammā' moreyiḍuvē

Entō tiraññu (Malayalam)

entō tiraññu eṅgum alaññu
onnum labhikkātirikke
enne marannu ellām maraññu
ninne ariññu ñān ammē - ñān
ninne ariññu ñān ammē

I was searching for something, I was wandering everywhere. Just when I thought I was not gaining anything, I forgot who I was, everything disappeared and I realized You Mother, I realized You.

ēkānta rāvukaḷ, ētō kināvukaḷ
entō tiraññuḷḷa tīrā ninavukaḷ
viṅgum hṛdayavum tiṅgunna cīntayum
vallāte ennuḷḷil vallāyma tīrtta nāḷ

Lonely nights and unclear dreams, constant memories of searching for something... With an aching heart and crowded thoughts, I felt extreme discomfort in my mind, in those days.

kaṇḍu ñān ammaye, kēvala mūrttiye
kēṭṭu ñān āsvaram kātinn-amṛtamāy
innumā nādam muzhuṅgiṭunnennuḷḷil
'amma ñān ennum, nī endetu mātram'

Then I saw Mother, the supreme Goddess. I heard that voice, like nectar in my ears. Even today, I hear that voice resonating inside me saying, 'I am Mother forever, you are mine alone.'

janmapuṇyamē jīvarāgamē
sarvamangaḷē sadgatipradē
varṣamēghamē prēmavarṣamē
divyadhāmamē dhanyavigrahē

Merit of many births, melody of life, most auspicious One, bestower of the right paths, cloud of rain, torrential rain of love, divine abode, divine form...

Ērēri ērēri (Malayalam)

ērēri ērēri ērēri ērēri
ērēri ērēri
teyyantārā takatimi
tāra takadhimi tāra takadhimi tāra takadhimi tā
taka tāra takadhimi tāra takadhimi tāra
takadhimi tā

Blissful joy. Beat of the drums

nīlakkārvarṇṇanām ōmanakkuṭṭane
cēlilāyannamma keṭṭiyiṭṭē
takadhimi
pālukavarnnaṅgu pāññupōm kaḷḷane
pāzhuralonnilāyi keṭṭiyiṭṭē
takadhimi

Darling child, with a dark blue color like clouds. Mother Yashoda caught her adorable dark blue child while he was stealing milk, and tied him up.

pīlittaṇḍonnu koṇḍ-ēṟeyaṭiccamma
cōranāy pōyille entuceyyām
takadhimi
pāriliṅgellārum pāṭēyurakkyunnu
tāya yaśōdatan kaḷḷan-ennu
takadhimi

She hit him with a peacock feather, how else could she deal with the 'little thief'? Everybody is going around singing about 'Mother Yasodha's little thief'.

cērivār cenkatir cōrunna vākkukaḷ
cālēyuraccitu kaṇṇanappōḷ
takadhimi
vārivariññiṭṭu vāṭippōy ñānammē
māyaṅgaḷentu ñān ceytatammē
takadhimi

Krishna addressed His mother, "I am tired. What mischief have I done for you to punish me like this?'

ādiyil nīyenne mārilāy bandhiccu
kātilāy kaḷḷan-ennōtiyillē
takadhimi
māmalapōluḷḷa kāruralonnilāyi
īvidham bandhiccu ippōrenne
takadhimi

"First you held me tight in your embrace and murmured 'thief' in my ear. Why have you tied me now against this cold hard stone mortar as big as a mountain?

māyaṅgaḷ colli nī mānasam māttaṇḍa
tēnūrum vākku ñān kēṭṭatetrā
takadhimi
vīṭukaṭannēri-pālukavarnnōnu
vīṭṭile kallural tannepōrum
takadhimi

"Please do not try to melt my heart with your sweet words to escape this punishment" mother replied, "Even if I have tied You to this mortar, You are smart enough to escape and steal the fresh milk in the evening from the homes of the Gopis."

pāśakkurukkukaḷ ētumazhiyāte
tāyayaṅgāśu pōyiṭum nēram
takadhimi
tāruviriyunna pōloru puñcirī
tāmarakkaṇṇan ninaccatentē
takadhimi

Without untying or loosening the rope, His mother left Him and went away. Krishna, the lotus-eyed Lord, gave a mischievous smile that resembled a blossoming lotus.

kallural tānē cummiyeṭuttiṭṭu
centāmarakkaṇṇan vīṭuviṭṭē
takadhimi
tan viralonnilāy māmalapokkuvōn
pāzhural ceṇḍupōl pokkukkillē
takadhimi

Krishna deftly and with ease pulled the stone mortar behind Him as He strolled out of His home. What is a stone mortar to the One who could lift up the huge mountain (Govardhana) with his child finger?

ārppuviḷiccukoṇḍambāṭi kuññuṅgaḷ
āyarkulōttamanoṭottu nīṅgi
takadhimi
āvazhikkaṅgāyi raṇḍu maruttukaḷ
kallural cērttavan taḷḷiyiṭṭu
takadhimi

A crowd of cheering children gathered and walked behind the Lord. Two tall trees obstructed His path and He uprooted them both as He passed between them dragging His stone mortar.

ā marajanmattin śāpamōkṣam
īyuga niścayam tanneyallī
takadhimi
nīlakkārvarṇṇande līlakaḷellāmē
īyuga niścayam tanneyallī
takadhimi

Thus were the two sons of Kubera liberated from their curse to live as trees until Lord Vishnu blessed them. These are the captivating stories of Lord Krishna, a part of His divine play in this world.

Gajamukha pūjita (Telugu)

gajamukha pūjita ṣaṇmukha sēvita
śritajana pōṣita paśupati dēvā
pārvatiramaṇā paramadayāḷō
śaraṇam śaraṇam śivapada kamalam

You are worshipped by the elephant-faced One (Ganapathi) and served by Muruga. You are the nourisher of those who surrender to You, and are the Lord of all creatures. O Consort of Parvati, You are the most compassionate One. O Lord Shiva, we take refuge at Your lotus feet!

namaḥ śivāyōm namaḥ śivāyōm
namaḥ śivāyōm namaḥ śivāyōm

Salutations to the most auspicious Lord Shiva!

digambara bhairava bhujanga bhūṣita
bhasmālankṛta candrābharaṇā
śmaśāna sadanā vairāgya sampada
śaraṇam śaraṇam śivapada kamalam

The sky is Your garment, O Bhairava, and snakes are Your ornaments. You are smeared with sacred ash, and the crescent moon adorns Your head. The cremation ground is Your abode, and You are the embodiment of dispassion. O Lord Shiva, grant us refuge at Your lotus feet!

trinētra mūrttiki nī mora ceppu
trilōkapāluḍu ēlaka pōḍu
trikālajñuḍu trikālātītuḍu
śaraṇam śaraṇam śivapada kamalam

Tell your problems to the God with three eyes. The ruler of the three worlds will protect you. Shiva knows all the three times (past, present and future) and is beyond them. O Lord Shiva, grant us refuge at Your lotus feet!

Gala gala (Telugu)

gala gala gājula savvaḍi
jhana jhana gajjala samdaḍi
paka paka navvula cinnadi
jaya līlā vinōdini
bālā tripurasundari

Bangles are jingling, 'gala, gala'; anklets are jingling, 'jhana jhana'. The little One is laughing 'paka, paka' (charming laughter)... Victory to the Goddess who delights in Her play! Victory to Bala Tripurasundari, the Divine Mother worshipped in the form of a magnificent little girl.

bommala sṛṣṭini cēsinadi
bommala tīgalu paṭṭinadi
jagamu līlagā naḍupunadi
tanatō tānē aḍutunnadi

She has made a creation of toys. She is holding the strings of toys. She is running the world like a play. She is playing only with Herself (none else is there to play with Her).

ahamanu māyatō kappinadi
māyanu vīḍi rammannadi
cikkadu dorakadu cinnitalli
dāguḍu muṭalu āḍutalli

She has covered everyone with the illusion of 'I', and is asking us to come out of that illusion. The little One can neither be caught nor found easily. She is playing hide and seek with everyone.

tallī pātranu āḍutunnadi
banḍatanamu camputunnadi
prēmanu manalō nimputunnadi
pillala manassu pōmdamannadi

Now She is playing the role of Mother. She is removing the rigidities of ignorance and arrogance within us. She is filling us with love. She wants us to develop the innocence of a child.

jaya līlā vinōdini
bālā tripurasundari

Victory to the Goddess who delights in Her play! Victory to Bala Tripurasundari!

Hara hara śivanē (Tamil)

hara hara śivanē karuṇāmayanē
jñānakkaṭalē śaraṇam

Shiva, the compassionate One, the ocean of knowledge, we seek refuge in You.

aṭimuṭi kāṇaśivanē - unakku
abhiṣēgankaḷ seyavōm
aḷantiṭa iyalā paramē unakku
azhagiya ātaigaḷ neyvōm
arivukkarivām arivē unnai
arintiṭa kaṇṇīr pozhivōm
anpukku vaśamāgum kanivē un
aṭimalar paṇindē uyvōm

Shiva, (whose neither beginning nor end can be seen,) we will perform abhishekam (ritual of worship) to You. You are the supreme One who doesn't waver, we will weave beautiful clothes for You. You are the repository of all knowledge, we will shed tears and yearn to know You. You are the merciful One who gives in to love alone, we will get liberated by worshipping Your Feet.

hara hara om namaḥ śivāya
bhava hara om namaḥ śivāya
śivāya namaḥ om
harāya namaḥ om
bhavāya namaḥ om
parāya namaḥ om

Our salutations to Hara, Shiva, Bhava, the Supreme One!

Hārati gaikonumā (Telugu)

hārati gaikonumā ammā
mangaḷārati gaikonumā ammā

O Mother, please accept our arati (homage) to You.

bhānuniki dīpamu avasaramā
mā madilō cīkaṭi māpammā
nī rūpamu yedalō veligincu
dīpāla hārati gaikonumā

Does the sun need the light of a lamp? Please dispel the darkness in our hearts and illumine it with Your divine presence. Please accept our arati of lights.

svayamugā karugutunainā
parulaku parimaḷamu pancēvu
ī guṇamu mā naijamavvāli
dhūpāla hārati gaikonumā

Like the burning incense stick, You spread fragrance all around. May we acquire this virtue. Please accept our incense arati.

śeṣamu lēśamainā migulaka
ahamunu pūrṇṇamugā kariginc u
nīlō pūrttigā līnamujēyu
karppūra hārati gaikonumā

When camphor burns away, it leaves no residue. May our ego be reduced to nothing, and may we thus become one with You. Please accept our camphor arati.

dīpāla hārati gaikonumā
dhūpāla hārati gaikonumā
karppūra hārati gaikonumā
mangaḷa hārati gaikonumā

Please accept our arati of lights. Please accept our incense arati. Please accept our camphor arati. Please accept our auspicious arati.

Hariyuva nadiya (Gujarati version)

khalla khalla vahetī nadīo bole
pyāru evu śiv nām
rāghav rāmanā hṛdaymā dhabke
har har har har har nām

kaṇ kaṇ mā che vās teno
jagtamā rame nām tenu
śiv śiv bhajile o man re
dekhile sarvamā te śivane

har om śiv om har om namaḥ śivāya
har om śiv om har om namaḥ śivāya

tāru māru ahī śu che
je che te ek śiv to che
śivmā gurune tu dekhile
gurumā śivne tu jāṇile
har om śiv om har om namaḥ śivāya

Har pal har kṣaṇ (Hindi)

har pal har kṣaṇ har ghaṭanā me
daras ho jāye terā
samajh na pāye viṣayom me rat
pagalā hai man merā - kanhā
pagalā hai man merā

May I have Your darshan in every moment, every second, every situation. O Krishna, my mind has become mad with the objects of the world.

tujh ko pāne kī khātir
kuch aur nahī karnā hai
apnā sārā boj tumhāre
carṇo me dharnā hai
tū uskā hi banjātā hai
jo ban jāye terā
dars ho jāye terā

To obtain You all one needs to do is offer their burdens at Your feet - You become theirs, they become Yours. Please grant me Your darshan...

tum to dayā ke sāgar ho prabhu
sādhu jan sab kahte
nām tumhārā jiske dil me
us dil me hī rahte
jyoti kiraṇ ban tum hi camakte
man me ho jo andherā
dars ho jāye terā

All the ascetics say You are the ocean of compassion. You reside in the heart where Your name is enshrined. When there is confusion and darkness in the mind, You become a shining ray of light. Please grant me Your darshan.

Jag janani (Punjabi)

jag janani tū de bhakti tū
bhay haruni tū de śakti tū
merī dāti tū de mukti tū

O Mother of the world, grant me devotion. Destroyer of fear, grant me strength. O my Mother, grant me liberation!

aj phir caḍeyyā sī sūraj
aj phir sūraj hai ḍubeyā
beṭhā sī uḍikā vicc
hanjūvā dī jyot layī

Today the sun has risen again, today the sun has set again. I sit here waiting, lighting the lamp with my tears.

pancī vī terā, nām pukkāraṇ
pavan vī sāh roke khaḍī huṇ
tāre vī paye hār baṇāvaṇ
daras tere nū tarasaṇ

Even the birds call your name, even the wind has stopped blowing. The stars have made a garland for You, yearning for a glimpse of You.

kinne hī me janam gavāye
māyā jāl vicc vāng machulī
e janam tere caraṇāvicc arupit
kare arddās e das

How many lives have I wasted playing hide and seek in this game of maya (illusion). This servant prays for this life to be offered at Your holy feet.

Jamunā ke taṭ par (Hindi)

jamunā ke taṭ
par nāce mohan
rādhā gopiyo ke sang

On the banks of the Yamuna, the enchanting One (Lord Krishna) danced with Radha and the gopis (milkmaids).

cāndnī rāt hai
phailī hai bāt ye
"kānhā calē khelne
rās unke sang"

On that moonlit night, there were whispers in Vraj that Krishna had gone to play the rasa lila with the gopis.

kānhā kē cintan
me khogayā man
hoṭoṅ me lete gayī
nām har kṣaṇ

With thoughts of Krishna in their minds and His name on their lips every moment,

gopiyā nācī bhūle tan man
khele divya rās hoke magan

The gopis danced with abandon, forgetting body and mind. Thus they became totally engrossed in the sacred rasa.

kānhā khele rās... rās rās rās... rās mahārās

This is the rasa that Krishna played, the great rasa.

ātmā paramātmā kā thā ye sanyōg
dekh-ke cakit rah gaye tīn lok

The rasa was the union of the jivatma (individual soul) and the paramatma (supreme soul). Seeing it, the denizens of the three worlds were amazed.

sāre jag bhūl gaye apnā śok
ānand me ḍubo diyā kānhāne sab kō

The whole world forgot its grief. The Lord of Vraj immersed everyone in bliss.

suddha hogaye jab tan man prāṇ
har gopīke pās ā khaḍe gopāl

When the gopis' body, mind and vital breath became purified, the divine cowherd came and stood next to each one of them.

bhakti se nāce ve sab ek sāth
ye thā kānhā kā adbhut mahārās

They danced and sang together. This was Krishna's amazing and great rasa.

Japonām japonām (Bengali)

rāmāya rāmabhadrāya rāmacandrāya mānase
raghu nāthāya nāthāya sītayā pataye namo namaḥ
japo śrīrām bhajo śrīrām gāvo śrīrām

Obeisance to Lord Sri Rama (the embodiment of the perfect son, friend, king - the ideal one), consort of Sita (Rama's wife – symbolizes all that is great and noble in womanhood)... Chant the name of Sri Rama, sing the name of Sri Rama.

japonām japonām japonām
japo śrīraghu rām
rām rājārām rām sītārām
rām rādheśyām rām jay jay rām

Chant the name of Lord Rama, Lord of the Raghu dynasty, King Rama, consort of Sita, Radheshyam...

amār monnette rām prānnettī rām
śob kicū tāyī rāghovo rām
amṛto madhuronām bhajo abhirām
paromo śānti śubh borive monno prāṇ

Our only true friend in life is Rama. In sorrow the One ever beside us is Rama. Chant the name of the Lord incessantly, your mind will be filled with eternal peace.

otī bālośālī dhanurdhārī rām
potito pāvvonno śītārām
śoronne lāo prabhu cāronne āśāyye
śarv pāp hore amṛto rām nām

The embodiment of strength is Lord Ram, who wields the bow (signifying His readiness to destroy evil and protect righteousness), consort of Sita, uplifter of the downfallen. The one who comes to the holy feet of the Lord is under His protection. The immortal name of Rama frees us from all sins.

jay jay rām rām rām
jay jay rām rām rām
jay jay rām rām rām jay jay rām

Victory to Lord Ram! Victory to Sita Ram!

Kāla bhairavā (Kannada)

kāla bhairavā jaya jaya kāla bhairavā
kāmēśvara sambhūta kāla bhairavā

Victory to Kala Bhairava (an incarnation of Lord Shiva), who emanated from Lord Shiva!

brahma garva bhanga gaida ugrasvarūpiyē
nāgābharaṇa bhūṣita śiva kāla bhairavā
śaktipīṭha rakṣakanē śyāmavarṇa haranē
chāyā hṛdaya nandana guru kāla bhairavā

Of ferocious form, Kala Bhairava removed Lord Brahma's ego. A snake adorns the neck of Kala Bhairava. Of dark complexion, He protects the abode of Devi. Kala Bhairava is Guru of Saturn.

sarva dharma pālaka sakala sampat kāraka
bhikṣāṭana mūrttiyē digambaranē
astikavaca-dhāriyē āpat nirmūlanē
sarvakṣētra pālakanē kāla bhairavā

He safeguards righteousness and is the cause of all wealth. Garbed in the four cardinal directions, He epitomizes the religious mendicant. Clad in the armor of bones, He wards off all dangers. Kala Bhairava is protector of all temples.

lōbha-mōha kōpa-tāpa śoka nāśakā
śvāna vāhana śambhu kāla bhairavā
kāśinātha darśanakē mārgadarśi kārakanē
kāla bhaya nivārakā kāla bhairavā

Remover of greed, delusion, anger, suffering and sorrow, Kala Bhairava has the form of Lord Shiva, and His vehicle is the dog. Without having the darshan of Kala Bhairava, one cannot enjoy the vision of the Lord of Kashi (Varanasi). He destroys the fear of death.

Kālam kanalu (Tamil version)

kālam kanalinai pozhikkiradu
jīvan taṇalirku tavikkiradu
vāzhvenum vīthiyil muḷḷum pūvum
vāri vidaiykkirudu
vidhiyinai yār manam ninaikkirudu
vidhiyinai yār manam ninaikkirudu

seydadirkkēttra palan varum nēram
sirittiṭuvōm cilar azhuvōm
vidhiyadan tīrppum vinaiyadan palanum
nizhalinai pōl pintoṭarum
nizhalinai pōl pintoṭarum

kāṇunkaḷ samamāy sukha-dukhankaḷ
kālattin kōlam idellām
anubhavam palavidhamākum - nāmō
anubhava sāṭcikaḷ āvōm
anubhava sāṭcikaḷ āvōm

āsaikaḷ neyyum piravittaḷaiyadu
aruttāl azhindiṭum tuyaram
ātmavicāra vazhiyinai tazhuvi
aṭaivōm paramānandam
aṭaivōm paramānandam

Kala nuṇḍi kala loniki (Telugu)

kala nuṇḍi kala lōniki
kalakālamu kadilē kavi
mēlukō! mēlukō! suprabhātam
nīku jñāna suprabhātam

O Poet, we move eternally from dream to dream. Arise and awake! Morning greetings- may the sun of wisdom dawn within you.

kannulu kāñcē kala okkaṭi
kannulu kānani kala okkaṭi
avi pagaṭi kalalu konni
rātri kalalu konni konni
rātri kalalu konni konni

One dream is dreamt with eyes wide open, and another with eyes closed. Some dreams are dreamt throughout the day, and others at night while asleep.

gatamunu tovvē kalalanni
bhavitanu allē kalalanni
manassu kalpanalē anni
kala alalu kallalu anni
kala alalu kallalu anni

Dreams either dwell in the past or imagine a future. They are all figments of the imagination. As they are all illusory, the dreams will vanish, like the waves of the ocean.

janma-janmalu kalalu kalalu
jagamu-jīvulu kalalu kalalu
satī sutulu kalalu kalalu
illu oḷḷu kalalu kalalu
illu oḷḷu kalalu kalalu

Births, the world and its beings, wife and children, house and body—all these are nothing but dreams!

kalalu evarikō telusukō?
nīvu evarivō telusukō?
telusukō! mēlukō! suprabhātam
nīku jñāna suprabhātam

Find out to whom these dreams occur. Inquire into who you are. Know yourself! Arise and awake! May the sun of wisdom dawn within you!

Kānalēkunnānu ammā (Telugu)

kānalēkunnānu ammā - kūnanu
karuṇatō daricērccavammā
karigēdi kṣaṇamani tarigēdi bratukani
marigēdi ahamani murigēdi svārthamani

Mother, I am unable to even see You. Please be compassionate on this child and take me into Your fold. Time is melting away, life is passing, my ego is burning me, my selfishness is making me rot.

kaṭikacīkaṭi dāri krūramṛgamula dāḍi
janmakarmamula ūbi dāṭa taramā talli

O Mother, the night is pitch dark, cruel animals attack me, please help me to cross over this cycle of life!

māṭa vinanī-manasu māya marmapu mūsugu
sahakariñcani-tanuvu karmaphalamula muḍupu

My heart doesn't listen to me. In the veil of the mysterious maya, this body of mine doesn't cooperate and I am caught in the bondage of my own karma and its results.

karuḍugaṭṭina ahamu kuriyaniyadu-kṛpanu
dikkevvarika nāku nā cēy vadalaku

My unmelting ego is not allowing Your grace to flow. Who else is there for me as refuge? Please never let go of my hand.

sarvamu nīvē jagadambā
caraṇamē śaraṇamu jagadambā

You are everything to me, O Goddess of the Universe. Your lotus feet are my sole refuge.

Kaṇṇā kaṇṇā kaṇṇā (Tamil)

kaṇṇā... kaṇṇā... kaṇṇā... ōṭi vā...
gānakkuzhal gītam pāṭi vā
ālilaiyin tūyinṭravā
akhilam - tanai kāttavā
vāri aṇaikkum karankaḷ pōttruvōm - emai
vāri aṇaikkum karankaḷ pōttruvōm

Krishna, come running to me, playing the flute. The One who slept on the banyan leaf, come and reveal Yourself to me. Let us praise the hands that embrace us.

vānam toṭṭu ninṭravanai
vaiyyam tanai aḷarndavanai
vāyinilē aṇḍamellām
tāyai kāṇa ceytavanē
vāri aṇaikkum karankaḷ pōttruvōm - emai
vāri aṇaikkum karankaḷ pōttruvōm

He is the One who touched the sky, the One who measured the world, the One who showed the entire Universe inside His mouth to His mother. Let us praise the hands that embrace us.

puḷḷil ēri parandavanai
bhūvulagam kāttavanai
eḷḷil nirai eṇṇaiyai pōl
enkum nirai mādhavanai
vāri aṇaikkum karankaḷ pōttruvōm - emai
vāri aṇaikkum karankaḷ pōttruvōm

He is the One who flew on a blade of grass, the One who protected the world. Like the oil in the sesame seed, He is the One who pervades everywhere. Let us praise the hands that embrace us.

rādhē rādhē kṛṣṇā rādhē rādhē...
rādhē rādhē kṛṣṇā rādhē rādhē...
kṛṣṇā kṛṣṇā... rādhā kṛṣṇā...

Kaṇṇā... un ninaivil (Tamil)

kaṇṇā... un ninaivil nān pāṭinēn - nittam
untanadu cindai vēṇḍinēn
kaṇgaḷ nanaikinṭratē kālkaḷ taḷarukinṭratē
kāṇumeṇṇum illaiyō kaṇṇā
kālam innum kaniyavillaiyō

Krishna, I sing immersed in thoughts of You. I pray that I think of You always. My eyes are wet with tears, my legs tremble and falter. When will I see you Krishna, has the time not yet come?

nīyum senṭra disai kaṇkaḷ kāṇumen kaṇṇā
ēkkam tānkavillaiyē kaṇṇai
tūkkam tazhuvavillaiyē
oraṭi vaikkayilē nūraṭikaḷ vaippavanām
kēṭṭatum uṇmayillayō kaṇṇā
kalmanam karaiyavillaiyō

Krishna, my eyes follow the direction you went in. My yearning is unbearable, I am unable to sleep. Is it not true that You come a hundred steps towards us if we take one step towards You? Has Your heart not melted yet?

inṭru en munnē vandiṭuvāy - urugum
en nilai kaṇṭiṭuvāy - taḷarum
ennaiyum tānkiṭuvāy - uyirum
un padam sērttiṭuvāy

Please come, appear before me today. See my plight, hold me as I falter and take my life which I offer at Your Feet.

Karīndra vadanā (Hindi)

karīndra vadanā ravīndu nayanā
surendra vinutā gaṇeśvarā
natārtti haraṇā
bhavābdhi taraṇā
tume hamārā praṇām hai

O elephant-faced One, Your eyes are as glorious as the sun, and You are worshipped by the lord of gods (Indra), O Ganesha... You destroy negativities and help us cross the ocean of transmigration, our salutations to You!

gaṇa nāyakā jaya gaṇādhīśā...
gaṇapati gaṇapati gaṇapati jay jay
girijātmajā sakaladeveśā...
gaṇapati gaṇapati gaṇapati jay jay
varadāna lōla sura vāgīsha...
gaṇapati gaṇapati gaṇapati jay jay
praṇavātmajā śivasutā vande...
gaṇapati gaṇapati gaṇapati jay jay

Victory to Ganapati, Lord of the ganas, son of Parvati, presiding deity of all the gods! Victory to You, giver of boons, eloquent Sage! Victory to Ganapati, Lord of the ganas. Obeisance to You, son of Shiva, You reside in the pranava mantra (Om).

paripāhi śrī gaṇeśa devā devā
pūjyapāda vāraṇāsyadeva
bālacandracūḍa nātha deveśā

Protect us Lord Ganesha, we worship Your holy feet. O elephant-faced One, You wear the crescent moon.

sitāro kā nāth kirīt terā
girīndr terā vihār hai
munīndr sārā tumāre cākar
hame bhī tere banāye dev

You wear a star-studded crown and reside in the mountains, served by all the sages. Please make us Yours also!

tumārī āgyā alamghya jo hai
karegi rāstā sugam sadā
hame tumārā pādābj hī hai
sadā sahārā vināyakā

Following Your commands will make our paths easy. Your holy feet are always our refuge.

jay jay gaṇeśa jay jay gaṇeśa

Victory to Lord Ganesha!

Kehendā hai mukh (Punjabi)

kehendā hai mukh
dil vi eho bōle
śaraṇ maiyyā dī paj paj āvō

My heart and words say: Come running and take refuge in Mother. Get absorbed in Mother's divine name.

mā nām vicch līn hō jāvō
jay mātādī jaykār bulāvō

Sing the praises of Mother and call out 'Victory to the Divine Mother!'

jay mātā dī jaykār bulāvō
jay mātā dī jaykār bulāvō

Victory to the Divine Mother!

lāgi lagan tere prem dī maiyyā
man hōyā bairāgi - mērā man hōyā bairāgi

O Mother, being absorbed in Your love, my mind has become withdrawn.

phikkē - paigayē dūjē ras sāre
anant prem dā pāgi - hōyā anant prem dā pāgi

All other pleasures have become tasteless after sipping the nectar of Your infinite love.

jad vī usārē ghar sukhān de
dukhān ne dittī tad tad dastak

Whenever I constructed the houses of happiness, sorrow knocked on the doors.

tere divya prem de mahal vicch maiyyā
dukh vī hō gaye nat mastak

However in the palace of Your divine love, even the sorrows bow down.

tū hī ādi tū hī ant maiyyā
vicch māyā dā sāgar maiyyā

You are the beginning and the end, in between is the boundless ocean of maya.

mere samarpaṇ dī
kiṣti maiyyā
baṇ nāvak tū karāde pār

Please be the boatman of my boat of surrender and help me cross this ocean of maya.

miṭ jāṇā hai vicch miṭṭī de
phir kyon tu pajdā jāve

I will perish in the dust one day, why am I still running for pleasures?

terī hī līlā dā paḍudā
huṇ kaun hōr bacāve

This is all a curtain of Your divine play, who can protect me other than You?

Ke rādhā mane tu (Gujarati)

ke rādhā mane tu śyāmne maḷāvi de
ke rādhā mane ghanaśyāmne maḷāvi de

O Radha, please take me to Krishna, take me to that Krishna whose complexion is as dark as the rain clouds.

śyāmsundar mukh
mor mukuṭ-dhārī
mīṭhi madhuri bansi bajāve
te bansi bajaiyāne
jasumatilāl kanaiyāne
ke rādhā mane bansi bajaiyāne maḷāvi de

He has a beautiful face with a dark complexion, He wears a peacock feather in the crown, He plays sweet melodies on his flute. Take me to that flute player. O Radha, take me to that flute player.

go dhenun cāre vālo
gopi sang rāce
maṭki phoḍe citcore
te citcorne
te naṭkhaṭ gvālne
ke rādhā mane te citcorne maḷāvi de

He takes the cows for grazing, He plays with the gopis, He breaks their pots and steals their heart. O Radha, take me to that stealer of hearts.

vāki teni vāsalaḍi
vāki kamar teni
vāki tenī hṛdayni ḍagar
te bāke bihārine
vṛndāvan sancārine
ke rādhā mane bāke bihārine maḷāvi de

He holds the flute crooked, His posture is not straight, the ways to reach his heart are not straight either! Take me to that most beautiful One whose ways are inscrutable. O Radha, take me to that most beautiful One.

ke rādhā mane tum śyāmne maḷāvī de
ke rādhā mane ghanaśyāmne maḷāvī de
ke rādhā mane bansī bajaiyāne maḷāvī de
ke rādhā mane te citcorane maḷāvi de
ke rādhā mane bāke bihārīne maḷāvi de

O Radha, please take me to Krishna, take me to that Krishna whose complexion is as dark as the rain clouds. Take me to that flute player. O Radha, take me to that most beautiful One.

Koṭānukoṭī (Gujarati version)

koṭānukoṭī varṣo thakī satyane
śodhī rahyo manuṣya... śodhī rahyo manuṣya

dhyānanimagn banī tārī divya dhārāmān
vahāvā nij ātmāne
saghaḷu tyajī ṛṣiśvaro te to
antarhit varṣo tapas kare...

ghorvātā janjāvātmān
sūryatejas sam jyot tārī
niścal banī jaltī rahe sadā
tāg teno koī kāḍhī nā śake...

puṣpa latāo, pūjānā sthāno
uttama nūtana mahā mandiro
yugonā yugathakī rāh jūe tārī
tu to kyaya dūre dūre...

Koyi sūṇe nā sūṇe (Gujarati)

koyi sūṇe nā sūṇe
tujthi nathi kayi aṇsuṇu
koyi jāṇe nā jāṇe
tujthi nathi kayi aṇjāṇu
koyi dekhe nā dekhe mā
tujthi nathi kayi andekhu

O Mother, whether anyone listens or not, nothing remains unheard by You. Whether anyone knows or not, nothing is unknown to You. Whether anyone looks or not, nothing remains unseen by You.

suṇu dukhiyonā dukh karu sahūni sahāy
evo bhāv amne āpo mā nissvārtth sevā
karvā tatpar te hāth, mā amne āpo

O Mother, grant us the attitude that will help us listen to the sorrows of others and help the needy. Grant us hands that are eager to serve others.

dekhu tujhne sahumā, karu sahuno ādar
evidṛṣṭi amne āpo hṛdaymā cabi tāri
mukhmā nām tārā ānkho mā tū ne tū

O Mother, grant us the sight that sees You in everyone and regards everyone with respect. In our hearts we hold Your vision, on our lips we hold Your name and in our eyes we hold only You.

Kṛṣṇā karuṇadi kṛpe (Kannada)

kṛṣṇā... karuṇadi kṛpe tōru
bēḍida varagaḷa nī nīḍū
nandakumārā navanītacōrā
vṛndāvana sañcāra kṛṣṇā

O Lord Krishna, graciously shower Your grace and bestow on me the boon I seek. You are the son of Nanda and a butter thief. You roam through Vrindavan.

krōdhavarjjita kaustubhadharanē
rādhāmādhava rājīvanētranē
yadukulatilaka yaśōdabālakā
madanamōhana śrī madhusūdana hari

You have conquered anger, O wearer of the kaustubha gem. O Lord of Radha, Your eyes are shaped like lotus petals. Scion of the Yadu dynasty and darling son of Yashoda, You are mesmerizing. You destroyed the demon Madhu.

dīnōdhāranē dēvakitanayanē
rādhāmanōhara rāsavilōlanē
gōparipālaka gokulanandanā
pāvanāmga hare pāṇḍuranga viṭhalā

O son of Devaki, You uplift the downtrodden. You captivated Radha's heart and enacted the famed rasa dance. You protected the cowherd clan and were the darling of Gokula. O pure-limbed One, You are also Panduranga Vitthala.

kṛṣṇa kṛṣṇa rādhā kṛṣṇa
kṛṣṇa kṛṣṇa rādhā kṛṣṇa
kṛṣṇa kṛṣṇa rādhā kṛṣṇa
kṛṣṇa kṛṣṇa rādhā kṛṣṇa

Kūgi karedē (Kannada)

kūgi karedē nānammā - nī
kāṇadādē hēgammā
āgadāgadu nannamma - innu
sahisalārenu nannammā

O my Mother, I have been calling out to You... Why is it that You are not to be seen? I am not able to bear this any longer, O Mother...

kaṇṇu tumbi bandarē nannammā
mana tumbi taruvē nīnammā
īga maretiruvudu yākammā - ninna
meccisuvudu atu hēgammā

O Mother if only You were to fill my eyes with the vision of You, if only You would fill my heart... Why have You forgotten me now? How can I attain You?

ninna pāda appi nānu karediruvē
nanna mana bayakeya nī tiḷidiruvē
tiḷidu tarede nī haṭa hiḍidiruvē
adaroḷagē yēnū nī bayasiruvē

Hugging Your feet, I am calling out to You, You know my heart's desire. Yet knowing it, You stubbornly withhold it. So what is it that You desire, O Mother?

ammā... heḷammā... ammā... bārammā...
ammā... heḷammā... ammā... bārammā...

O Mother, tell me Mother! Come to me, O Mother!

Mahāmahima (Kannada)

mahāmahima ḷiruvē nī
makuva moreya kēḷu nī

O Mother, embodiment of greatness, please listen to this child's plea.

paruṣa rasa vidyekaḷali
pravīṇe yāda dēvi nī
prēma karuṇe sparśa nīḍi
cinnavāgisu enna nī

You are the master of all forms of knowledge. Embrace me with Your divine touch and purify me like gold.

sṛṣṭi marmma arita māye
tapōnidhi tāyi nī
śuddha bhakti jñāna nīḍi
prasāda vāgisu enna nī

You are the Mother of devotion who knows the secret of Creation. Bestow me with pure devotion and knowledge and make me a boon to Creation.

parama padada sīmeyalli
virājamāna guruvu nī
śaraṇu śaraṇu bhāva nīḍi
dhūḷi yākisu enna nī

You are the teacher who guides us in the eternal journey of life. Give me the attitude of surrender and transform me into dust at Your lotus feet.

Manasā vācā (Marathi version)

manasā vācā karmaṇā
nirantar smarito tujalā
kā bare hā vilamba ā ī
dayā dākhaviṇyā majavarī

kitī varṣe aśī sarlī
nase svasthatā mājhyā manī
alpaśī sāntvanā de māte
kā bare hā vilamba ā ī
kā bare hā vilamba ā ī

ā ī maj asahya jhāle
nako maj he ase jīvan
aśakta mī tav parīkṣā jhelaṇyā
malā ātā he asahya jhāle
malā ātā he asahya jhāle

vādaḷī phasalelyā tārusam
bharakaṭṭale g man māze
bhramiṣṭa na hovo he jīvan
thoḍītarī de śāntī mazalā
thoḍītarī de śāntī mazalā

ambe mī nirādhār jagatī
tujavin nase kuṇī mazalā
thāmbavī tujhī parīkṣā ātā
de ūnī kar, ghe maj javaḷī
de ūnī kar, ghe maj javaḷī

Mayil pīlī (Malayalam)

mayil pīlī tūlikayākki
harināma mantraṅgaḷ ezhuti
mazhavillin varṇṇaṅgaḷāle
ezhuti nin citraṅgaḷ-ēre

I wrote names and mantras of Hari using a peacock feather as a pen. I drew many pictures of You using colors of the rainbow.

arayālilakaḷ calikkē
kēḷkkunnita-ramaṇi kilukkam
mazhamukil vānil parakkē
kāṇmu nin śyāmaḷarūpam
kāṇmu nin śyāmaḷarūpam

As the leaves of the banyan tree move, we hear Your sweet tinkling sound. As the rainy dark clouds spread across the sky, we see Your divine blue form.

kṛṣṇa hare jaya kṛṣṇa harē
kṛṣṇa hare jaya kṛṣṇa harē
kṛṣṇa hare jaya kṛṣṇa harē
muraḷi manohara kṛṣṇa harē

Victory to Krishna! Krishna the flute player who captures our hearts.

muraḷiyil ozhukum rāgam
hṛdayamatil pakarum rāgam
māyilla hṛttil īdṛśyam
kāṇuvator apūrva puṇyam
kāṇuvator apūrva puṇyam

Melodies flowing through the flute, spreading to the heart. This vision will never vanish from the heart. It is a rare blessing for those who see it.

Nā guṇḍe (Telugu)

nā guṇḍe guḍilōna koluvuṇḍi pōvammā
muggarammalaku amma mūlapputamma

Be enshrined in the temple of my heart, O Primordial Mother who is the basis of the three goddess mothers (Saraswati, Lakshmi and Parvati).

pāla sandramu paina maṇidvīpamanduna
padmavanamula centa cintāmaṇula inṭa
śatakōṭi sūryula kāntulu prabhaviñca
koluvu tīrē talli śrīmātā śrīlaḷitā

On a bejewelled island in the ocean of milk, in the lotus forest, in the house made of wish-fulfilling gems spreading the light of a hundred crores of suns, You are enshrined, O Sri Mata, Sri Lalita.

śaktisēnalu kōtlu bhaktitō sēvimpa
iruvaipula cēri ramavāṇi koluvaṅga
paramēṣṭhi hariharulu pādālu tākanga
surajanulu jaya dhvanulu lōkāle mārmoga

Crores of armies of shaktis serve You with devotion. Standing on either side of You, Goddesses Lakshmi and Saraswati serve You with love. The trinity (Vishnu, Shiva and Brahma) touch Your lotus feet. The worlds resound with calls of victory led by gods and men.

sankalpa mātrāna sṛṣṭī kramamu naḍacu
kanureppa saigalatō kālacakramu tirugu
nī māya sṛjiyiñcu janamṛti valayālu
nī karuṇa teripiñcu kaivalya dvārālu

By Your will the Universe is created. The movement of Your eyelids turns the wheels of time. Your maya (illusion) weaves the web of life and death. Your compassion opens the doors of liberation.

Nāṭakam onṭru (Tamil)

nāṭakam onṭru naṭakkiradu
navarasam adilē irukkiradu
tānē ezhudi naṭikkum paramporuḷ
tannaiyē naṭippinil marakkiradu

A drama is happening, the nine rasas are in it. The supreme One is writing it as well as acting in it. It forgets itself in the act.

viṣayattil sukhamena ninaikkiradu
viḷakkankaḷ palappala tarugiradu
vidhivazhi senṭru taḷarndapin tānē
viṣam adu enṭru uṇargiradu

It thinks that there is happiness in material things. And gives many excuses to support it. Only after going through the fate and suffering does it understand that it is poisonous.

viraktiyil manamum tuvaḷgiradu
vilaṅginai arukka tuṭikkiradu
viṭaiyinai kāṇum muyarcciyil arivu
vinaviya tannai paṭhikkiradu

The mind despairs in frustration. It craves to break free from bondage. The intellect, in pursuit of finding an answer, tries to find the self that raised the question.

kaḷḷattai kaṇḍupiṭikkiradu
uḷḷadai sariyāy arigiradu
nāṭakam enṭṛu arindapin iduvarai
naṭandadai eṇṇi cirikkiradu

It understands time and things as they are. After realizing that it is all a drama, it laughs at what has happened.

Nīlāmbuja nayane (Gujarati version)

nīlāmbuja nayanā ammā
jāṇyā te śu ā duhkhī haiyāna duḥkhaḍā

kevā janmonā karmo kerā
bhatkī rahiyo hū eklo āj

yugo na yugthaki āvī rahiyo hū
ā yuga sandhyāmā pharī janamyo
bolāvile pāse tārī rākh mane

tārā khoḷāmā poḍāḍi de - ammā
tārā khoḷāmā poḍhāḍi de

yogya ā putra nathī pūche mātā ne
tyajaśe śū tene ā kāje

āvo mā mane haiyye lagāvo
tārī kṛpā mā seje vahāvo... ammā
tārī kṛpā mā seje vahāvo

Nīlāmbuja nayane (Tamil version)

nīlattāmarai vizhiyāḷē ammā - nī ariyāyō
nīrumen neñcattin vēdanaikaḷ
ēdō piraviyil seydadōr seyalāl
tanimaiyilē nān tavikkinrēn

yugamyugamāka nīnti kaṭantu nān - inta
yugattilum pirantu vantēn
azhaippāyō aḷḷi aṇaippāyō
un maṭiyil iṭam koṭuppāyē ammā...
un maṭiyil iṭam koṭuppāyē

takutiyillenṭrālum tāyum tan makkaḷai
kaiviṭuvāḷō tāriṇiyē
varuvāyē arukil aṇaippāyē
unnaruḷ mazhaiyil nanaippāyē ammā
unnaruḷ mazhaiyil nanaippāyē

Nirmala jīvana (Kannada)

nirmala jīvana nīṭite nī
karmavellā aḷiside nī
karuṇēya kantā nānāde bindu
amṛtānanda sindhu
amṛtānanda sindhu

You have given me a pure life. You have wiped away all karma. I, a child of compassion, have become the ocean of immortal bliss.

śaraṇāgatiya kalisutali
cirasukha mārgava tōrite nī

ānandakantā nānāteyindu
pāvana vāyitu jīvana
jīvanavāyitu pāvana

By teaching me surrender, You have shown me the path to eternal happiness. Today I have become a child of bliss. My life is now fulfilled.

nintaratē ninna sānnidhyavammā
kuntāka ninna dhyānavammā
naṭevāka ninna nāma sangāti
malakitarē atē namaskāra
malakitarē atē namaskāra

Right where I am standing is where Your presence is. When I sit, it is in meditation on You. As I walk, Your name is my companion. My lying down to sleep is a prostration to You, O Mother.

Oṭa kuzhalūti (Malayalam)

oṭa kuzhalūti vā vā
kaṇṇa vṛndāvana bālā
onnu kāṇiccu tarāmo
ninde divya rūpam

Playing the flute, please come, O Krishna, boy of Vrindāvan. Please show me Your divine form.

tāmara kaṇṇukaṇḍoṭṭe
pīli-tirumuṭi toṭṭoṭṭe
pitāmbaram cuttiya uṭalonnu
kaṇḍu ñān rasikkaṭṭe
kaṇḍu ñān rasikkaṭṭe

Please let me see Your lotus eyes, and let me touch Your hair adorned with a peacock feather. Let me delight in gazing at Your waist adorned with the yellow silk garment.

vaijayanti mālayum
mārile kaustubhavum
nin kamala pādaṅgaḷum
onnu ñān cumbiccoṭṭē
onnu ñān cumbiccoṭṭe

Wearing a garland of wild flowers, Your chest adorned with the kaustubha gem... Please let me kiss Your lotus feet.

pullankuzhalūti nṛttamāṭu kaṇṇā
ānandattil nin nāmam colli
onnu vaṇaṅgaṭṭe
onnu vaṇaṅgaṭṭe

Playing the bamboo flute, dance, O Krishna! Please allow me to bow before You, chanting Your name in a state of bliss!

Paritiyinmun paniyai (Tamil)

paritiyinmun paniyai pōlē
maraintiṭumē innalkaḷ tāyē
unnaruḷum kiṭaittuviṭṭāl
naṭavātatu ētum uṇḍō

Just like the fog that vanishes when the Sun comes out, our troubles disappear in Your presence. With Your grace, nothing is impossible.

tanvalimai periyatu enṭru
ātuvatum ettanai āṭṭam
unnaruḷin valimai uṇarntāl
ātuvarō ānava āṭṭam

We live, thinking that our potential is great. If we realize Your potential is unlimited, would we live with so much ego?

tannalattāl arivum mayanki
unperumai marantiruntēn
tanai marantu makkaḷai kākkum
tāyē karam piṭittiṭuvāy

I forgot Your greatness because my intellect is clouded by selfishness. O Mother, You forget Yourself and protect Your children; please hold my hand.

tanaipazhippōr tamaiyum aṇaikkum
dayaimikunta tāyē umaiyē
eṇṇilāta tavarukaḷ seytēn
mannittenai āṇḍaruḷvāyē

O merciful Mother Uma, You embrace even those who demean You. I have committed countless mistakes. Please forgive me and take over my life.

Paurṇṇamirāvil (Kannada version)

paurṇṇami rātri bānanu beḷaguva
pūrṇṇa candira nīnallavē amma?
sundara hūgaḷa gandhadi suḷiyuva
vasantagānavu nīnallavē amma?

tambūri tantiyu candadi miḍiyuva
impina rāgavu nīnallavē amma?
kavigaḷa sundara kalpanā lōkada
sumadhura kaviteyu nīnallavē amma?

sumadhura kaviteyu nīnallavē
ēḷubaṇṇadalu ēḷū svarādalu
ontāgi nalivaḷu nīnallavē ammā?
hūvina gandhavu maḷebillandavu
gāḷiya tampū nīnallavē amma?
tangāḷi tampū nīnallavē?

Paurṇṇamirāvil (Telugu)

paurṇami rātrilō ningilō veligē
candruni vennela nīvammā - ammā
candruni vennela nīvammā
suvāsanlolīkke pūlaḍōlilō vēcē
vasanta rātrivi nīvammā - ammā
vasanta rātrivi nīvammā

tambura mṛdu tantrilō pongēḍi
sundara nādam nīvammā - ammā
sundara nādam nīvammā
kavula kalpana ūala lāṭē
sumadhura gānam nīvammā - ammā
sumadhura gānam nīvammā

ēḍūrangulu ēḍu svarālū
okkaṭai cērēdi nīlōnē - ammā
okkaṭai cērēdi nīlōnē
pūvulō vāsana harivillantamu

gālilō callana nīvammā - ammā
gālilō callana nīvammā

Prati lēdu (Telugu)

prati lēdu nī prēmaku jagajjanani saritūgarū nīkevvarū
trilōkālalōnū trikālālalōnū saritūgarū nīkevvarū

There is no equivalent to Your love. You have no equal in all the three worlds and all the three times (past, present and future).

ellalerugani prēma kallalerugani karuṇā
dūramerugani ūta bēdhamerugani rakṣa
sāṭilēnēlēni mātṛvātsalyamu
prati lēdu nī vāsiki
jagatpālini saritūgarū nīkevvarū

Your love knows no borders, and Your compassion, no falsehood. Distance is no barrier to Your support, and Your protection does not discriminate. There is no equivalent to Your motherly affection. Your fame is unequalled, and You have no equal.

prēmayē pāśamu prēmayē karavālamu
prēmatō gelicēvu andarī manasulanu
prēmatō śilalanu malicēvu śilpālugā
prati lēdu nī śailiki
mahāśilpi saritūgarū nīkevvarū

Love is both Your binding cord and Your sword. You win everyone's heart with love, and in the heart You sculpt a rock into shape. Your style has no equivalent, You have no equal.

tēnakai tummedalu cērunu pūvu cuṭṭū
surāsurulu narula kūḍā gumigūḍedaru
paridhi lēnī valayāniki kēndramu nīvu
prati lēdu nī vaśamuku
jagatkāriṇi saritūgarū nīkevvarū

Just as bees gather around a flower for nectar, gods, demons and human beings gather around You. You are the centre of a circle without a circumference. Your attractiveness has no equivalent, You have no equal.

Rādhārāṇī ke pyāre (Hindi)

he kṛṣṇa, karuṇāsindho, dīnabandho jagatpate...
gopeśa gopikākānta rādhākānta namostute
namostute

O Krishna, compassionate One, friend of the destitute, Lord of the world, Lord of the gopas, beloved of the gopis, beloved of Radha, we prostrate to You.

rādhārāṇī ke pyāre ghanaśyām
bole rādhā se gāve nāce ham
tīnon lokon ke vāsī mugdh ho
bole milke sab 'rādhe rādhe śyām'

O Krishna with the complexion of a raincloud, You are the beloved of Radha. Let us sing and dance along with Radha. You live in the three worlds, You are so beautiful. Let's all say together 'Radhe Radhe Shyam.'

sab gvālon ne ākar diyā sāth
rāskelī me hone lagā śor
jayjay kāron se gūnjā sārā lok
rādhe rādhe śyām jay jay rādhe śyām

All the cowherd boys were with You, there was blissful celebration in the rasa dance. The whole world was resounding with the chant, 'Victory, victory!'. O Radhe Shyam! Victory to Radhe Shyam!

bole rādhe rādhe rādhe rādhe rādhe ghanaśyām
rādhe ghanaśyām... jay
rādhe ghanaśyām... jay
rādhe ghanaśyām... jay
rādhe rādhe rādhe rādhe rādhe ghanaśyām

Sing 'Radhe Radhe Ghanashyam'! Victory to Radhe Ghanashyam!

vṛjbhūmi kā mānas uṭhā jāg
jamunā se āyī mṛdul āvāz
phulvārī ke phūl khilke ḍol
nāce 'rādhe śyām' bole barse

The whole of Vrindavan awakened, the Yamuna river flowed melodiously, flowers bloomed and showered saying 'Radhe Shyam is dancing.'

Rām nām ras (Hindi)

rām nām ras taj kar manuvā
dūje ras apnāye
choḍ amararatā dhām yah paglā
janmon men bhaṭkāye

Abandoning the sweet name of the Lord, this mind has adopted other pleasures. Leaving behind the abode of Immortality, our delusion keeps us wandering and lost in the relentless cycle of birth and death.

duśman apnā merā hī man
kis par doṣ lagāvū
rām kī naiyyā ṭhukrā kar me
khud hī ḍūbā jāvū
dvār khulā hai prabhu kī dayā kā
isko nazar na āye
manuvā dūje ras apnāye
janmon men bhaṭkāye

When the enemy is my own mind, who is there for me to blame? Rejecting the Lord who would carry me across, I am seeking only to drown myself. The doors to the Lord's compassion are always open, yet this mind doesn't see it. Adopting other pleasures, it keeps us wandering and lost in the relentless cycle of birth and death...

nāmāmṛt hī madhur hai jag me
śeṣ sabhī zaharīle
mān sarovar choḍ ke mūrakh
kyon pīve jal maile
kṣaṇ kṣaṇ me caltā apne ko
mṛg tṛṣṇā me jāye
manuvā dūje ras apnāye
janmon men bhaṭkāye

The only sweet thing in the world is the nectar of the Lord's Name - all the rest is poison. O foolish mind, why do you insist on drinking dirty water when you could be drinking from the eternal pool of bliss of your Self? Burning every moment in unending desires, adopting other pleasures, it keeps us wandering and lost in the relentless cycle of birth and death...

bolo rām rām rām
sīyā rām rām rām

Chant the name of Rama, chant the name of Sita Rama!

Samsāraduḥkha (Telugu version)

samsāraduḥkha śamanam cēyyū
priyamaina lōkajananī
nī divyahasta caluvē satatam
satatam māku abhayam

andhatvamulō munigē jīva
bṛndānikamma śaraṇam
āpadalō māku abhayam - amma
nī pādapadma smaraṇam

sāntam bhramiñci hṛdayam - ghōra
timiramlō cikki tirigē
ī dusthitīki śamanam - amma
nī nāmarūpa mananam

sandīptalōla nayanā - lēnu
nā mānasamnu kadipe
nī pādapadmam cēra - adi
okkaṭṭē māku mārgam

Śankaranandana (Hindi)

śankaranandana pankajalocana
sankaṭmocana mangaḷadāyaka
dantikaḷebara santata sundara
sindhura nāyaka siddhivināyaka

O son of Shiva, lotus-eyed One, remover of troubles, One who brings auspiciousness. O Siddhi Vinayaka, the elephant-faced One, leader of elephants, who is eternally beautiful...

ādiganeśvara bhūtividhāyaka
mañjuḷa mānasa mattagajānana
mūṣikavāhana vighnavibhañjana
vandita nandita candana bhūṣita
gaṇanāthā śubhadātā vardātā he jagannāthā

O Ganesha, giver of prosperity, the One with a beautiful heart, O Gajanana, who rides the mouse as a vehicle, destroyer of obstacles, we salute You, O Lord of the ganas, giver of goodness and boons, O Lord of the worlds!

gaṇapati jay jay boliye
surapati jay jay boliye
śivsuta jay jay boliye
sukhakara jay jay boliye

Victory to the Lord of the ganas, victory to the Lord of the gods, victory to the son of Shiva, victory to the giver of happiness!

adbhutabālaka viśrutavikrama
nirjjara pūjita nirguṇa niścala
vāraṇa vigraha vānchita dāyaka
dānava dāraṇa nīrada śyāmaḷa
gaṇanāthā śubhadātā vardātā he jagannāthā

O marvellous child, the One with great strength who is worshipped by the Gods. You are beyond the gunas (qualities), You are unmoved and have the form of an elephant. You grant the wishes of the devotees, and are the destroyer or demons. O Lord of the ganas, giver of goodness and boons, O Lord of the worlds...

Śaraṇennirō (Kannada)

śaraṇennirō ammana pādake śaraṇu ennirō
jñānāmṛta guruvina pādake śaraṇennirō

Salutations to the feet of the Divine Mother; salutations to the feet of the Guru, who showers the nectar of knowledge on us.

niṣkalanka bhāva nimma nijaguṇa kāṇirō
nirmala prema nimma nijarūpa ariyirō
nijānanda paḍeyalu nijātmava tiḷiyirō
nīnē ellā nānēnu allā
nīnē ellā nānēnu allā
nīnē ellā ninē ellā... ammā
nīnē ellā nānēnu allā
nīnē ellā nānēnu allā ennuta śaraṇennirō
ammana pādake śaraṇennirō

Through the pure state She is established in, She will help you know your real nature. Through Mother's love, discover your true Self. To gain eternal bliss, know your Self. You are everything, O Mother, I am nothing. Take refuge at Mother's feet with the attitude 'Mother You are everything, I am nothing'.

māḍuva karmā vellā ninnadamma ninnadu
nōḍuva nōṭṭa vellā ninnadamma ninnadu
kēḷuva daniyū ellā ninnadamma ninnadu
āḍuva nuḍiyū ellā ninnadamma ninnadu
ammana pādakke śaraṇennirō

All my actions are offerings to You, all that I see is Your vision. The voice that I hear is only Yours, what I speak is all Your words. Salutations at the lotus feet of the Divine Mother.

śaraṇennirō! nīvu
śaraṇennirō! īka
śaraṇennirō! bēka
śaraṇennirō!

Let us surrender, let us surrender now, let us surrender fast!

Seyda seyalgaḷ (Tamil)

seyda seyalgaḷ yāvum sattrē ninaindiḍu manamē - adil
seyda tīya seyalgaḷ eṇṇi varundiṭu manamē
varundi nīyum tirundi pudidāy pirandiṭu manamē - ini
varuvadellām iraivan seyalenṭrirundiṭu manamē
ō manamē... nī ninai manamē

O mind, reflect upon the actions you have performed and repent for the evil deeds. O mind, gain a new birth through rectifying your past mistakes and henceforth accept whatever comes as God's will. Reflect upon that, O mind.

pārvai manki ceviyaṭaikkum andi nērattil -
pāzhum
mūcc tiṇari pēcc kuzharum anda nērattil
kāladēvan kaṇakkai tīrkka kāttiruppānē - undan
kaṇṇakkaikkūṭṭi kazhiññu pārkka avan siripānē...
undan
kaṇṇakkaikkūṭṭi kazhiññu pārkka avan siripānē
ō manamē... nī ninai manamē

At the time when vision starts to dim, ears become deaf, breath stutters and speech loses its power. The god of death is waiting to close your account, he laughs looking at your balance. Reflect upon that, O mind.

sērndirunda yārum kūṭa varuvadum illai - palanāḷ
sērttu vaitta yāvum udava pōvadum illai
pārttu naṭandu paṭinda karaiyai kazhuviṭu
manamē - anda
paraman pādam pattri sugamāy irundiṭu manamē
anda
paraman pādam pattri sugamāy irundiṭu manamē
ō manamē... nī ninai manamē

None of your loved ones nor your possessions will accompany you at the time of death. O mind, tread carefully and get established in that supreme state which is bliss itself. Reflect upon that, O mind!

Śrī laḷitāmbikē sarvaśakte (Kannada version)

śrī laḷitāmbikē sarvaśakte
śrī laḷitāmbikē sarvaśakte
śrī laḷitāmbikē sarvaśakte
śrīpādakalamakē namisuvē nā

vaśadali illavammā dhyānarūpavu
niśēyali kaḷedide enna kālavu
animiṣa ennanu agalatē nī
hṛdayati entigu beḷagu ammā

nīṭamma enagē sadguṇa sarvā
śaraṇāgi bantihē duḥkhitē nā
punaḥ punaḥ māṭuve praṇāma ninakē
lavalēśa kāruṇya tōru amma

kaṭegaṇṇi lomme nī enna nōḍū
khedakaḷellavā marēsu dēvi
ninnaya dāsiyā porēyē dēvī
duḥkhamukte yākalu ēnu māḍali?

bēḍabēḍammā nī kai biḍabēḍā
śaraṇārthi makuvanū svīkarīsū
gamanavu ninneṭē munnaṭēsū
gati bērēyillā śaraṇu ammā

sarvābhīṣṭa pradāyinī nī
karuṇeya tōrū maheśi bhadrē
nama navā māṭalū śakti nīḍū
manamantiradali nṛtyamāṭū

akhilāṇḍa jyōtiyē divyamūrttiyē
agatigē gati nīḍū bhakti nīḍū
akhilaru ennanū dūṣisitarū
abhayavu nī mātra lōkamātē

nūrāru janmā kaḷētavēnō
hareyava marttyanantē kaḷetenēnō
viraḷavī janma manuṣyajanmavā
padapatma vandanekē mīsaliṭuvē

pāpakaḷēsō māḍiruvē nā
atipāpi nānū nintyaḷammā
janani nī ennanū kṣamisa lāreyā
manatāpavellavā aḷisa lāreyā

jñānavō śāstravō yōgavō hā
enakontū tiḷidillā tiḷiyadēnū?
karmada marmasahā tiḷiyatā ī
makuva ni āṭisuvē ētakammā?

ontiṣṭu niṣṭheyā pālisalu nā
dhyānakke kaṇmuccī kuḷittirūvē
nī bantu vicalitā vāgisitēyā
ucitavē ninnāṭṭā śiśuvinontikē

tāyiyu tanteyū guruvu ninē
manavṛkṣa puṣpaphala nīnammā
nenappukaḷellā ninnadāgalī
karuṇe tōru ammā kaimugīvē

nī namma tyajisī hōdeyātare
uḷivudu vyatheyē namma pālikē
arekṣaṇa ninnanu agali iralu
namagantu sahisalu āgadammā

nīnallatē bērē - yāru enagē
nīne yenna śvāsa niśvāsavammā
ninnanu akalī dūravākalū
nanagantū alpavū āgatammā

ninnanu toredu iralārenammā
arekṣaṇa kūṭā... sahissalārē
nī enna marēttū dūra hōtarē
ninnanu huḍukutā bhrāntaḷākuvē

cintekaḷellavū ninna cintēyē
karmakaḷellavū ninna pūjēyē
madhuranāma japipē adhara tumbī
nī mātra venakē sarvasva tāyē

iṣṭudina kaṇkaṭṭī āṭṭavāṭitē
inttha āṭṭavēnū bēḍa tāyē
nī enna śvāssavē ādeyammā
nī enna prāṇadā prāṇavādē

enna hṛtspandanā ninnalli ammā
enna cinte ninnā oṭali noḷakē
nāniruvē tāyī nina maṭilalī
lālippada hāḍalū mareyadiru nī

Śyām-golok-me (Hindi)

śyām-golok-me rās-bihārī
gokul me giridhārī
gokul me giridhārī

O beautiful Krishna from the land of cows, You revel in the divine dance, and lifted the Govardhan Mountain to protect Your devotees.

rāg rasīlā gān surīlā
rās lolupā karuṇālo
yādava rājā gokula pālā
gopījana priya śyāmā

You play melodious tunes on the flute and love the divine dance, O compassionate One. King of the Yadavas, divine cowherd, beloved of the cowherd girls.

bolo kṛṣṇ jay rādhā kṛṣṇ jay
gopīkṛṣṇ kṛṣṇ kṛṣṇ kṛṣṇ kṛṣṇ jay

Victory to Krishna, victory to Radha Krishna!

bāsurī tūne mohak pyāre
rās kelī me bajāyi
vyākul gopī dauḍ ke āyī
tere pago me kanayyā

You played enchanting tunes for the rasa-lila dance, the eager, yearning gopis came running to Your feet.

Tannanna tannanna (Malayalam)

tannanna tannanna tannanna tannanna
tannanna tannanna tānannā
tannanna tannanna tannanna tannanna
tannanna tannanna tānannā

kuttikozhiccuḷḷa tāvalavalini
keṭṭipotiññiṭṭu pōkaṇam
kēṭṭarivuḷḷa madhurāpurikkini
keṭṭariññaṅg-cennettaṇam

I shall take a handful of pounded raw rice in a small bundle. I must travel to the Kingdom of Madhura of which I have only heard about.

kālarivillātta dūramoṇennālum
nāvilāy nāmamuṇḍennumē
nārāyaṇā hare nārāyaṇā harē
nārakīyāganiyil kākkaṇē

Even though my legs do not know the way, my heart resounds with His name- 'Narayana Hare Narayana Hare!' Protect me from the misery of this world.

kuṭṭicceruppattilkkaṇḍuḷḷa kaṇṇane
kāṇmatiṅgippozhinnorkkavē
uḷḷam virakkyunnu tuḷḷituḷambunnu
kaṇṇunirayunnatentinō

I knew Krishna when He was very young. I am going to see Him again now, my heart is trembling with anticipation. When shall I see You again, my Lord?

vēgam naṭakkunnu kālukaḷentitu
kālam pazhayatinnōrkkayō
nārāyaṇā harē nārāyaṇā harē
kāṇukil nīyenneyōrkkumō

'O legs of mine! Walk fast, do not tarry, for I fear that it has been too long since we met.' 'Victory to Narayana! Will You remember me when we meet?

gōpuradvāram kaṭakkunnanērattu
gōvindan eṅgannu nōkkavē
nēreyaṇayunnu nārāyaṇan tānum
nāriparivāram-oppamāy

As I entered the magnificent palace gates, Govinda looked straight at me. I stood there absorbed in the sight of Narayana. He was standing there with His consorts.

keṭṭippiṭiccaṅg kātilāyōtunnu
ettuvān vaikiyatentu nī
nārāyaṇā hare nārāyaṇā hare
nīyariyāttatāyentinī

He came to me and hugged me tight; He whispered in my ear, 'Why did you delay so long in coming to me?' Victory to Narayana! What is there in this world that You do not know?

kāḷukazhukiccu kaiyyilpiṭicciṭṭu
cālēyakattekkyupōnnitā
talpattilāyitā oppamirikkavē
kaṇṇuniraññatumentinu

He washed my tired feet and took my hand in His. He escorted me inside and laid a seat for me. He sat beside me and His eyes welled up with tears.

tāmarakkaṇṇande kaṇṇuniraññatu
rugmiṇidēviyum kaṇḍuvō
nārāyaṇā harē nārāyaṇā hare
ninneyariññavarāruṇḍu

Why did my Lord Krishna's eyes well up with tears? Was He searching for Rukmini Devi? Victory to Narayana! Who is there in this world who has ever known You?

pāzhavilkkeṭṭatu kaiyyileṭukkunnu
pinneyum pinneyum nōkkunnu
pāṭṭilkkazhiccatāyitōnnumō
yillinitaṭṭikkuṭaññā lumonnumillā

The Lord looked again and again at the bundle of old and stale beaten rice flakes that I clutched in my hands. Will He think that I have eaten some of it? No, He is taking it from my hands.

pāribharikkunna tamburānāyoru
pāzhtuṇikkeṭṭē kaiyyiluḷḷu
nārāyaṇā harē nārāyaṇā harē
nīyariyāttatāyentinī

The Lord who is ruling this world is now holding a handful of stale flattened rice in a bundle made up of an old torn cloth. Victory to Narayana! What is there in this world that You do not know?

keṭṭuturakkunnu pāramkotiyōṭe
pāzhaviluṇṇunnu śauriyum
tāvala vilalla tāvaka
snēhamāṇennumenikkatu priyamām

He opened the bundle and looked at my offering. He started eating with great relish and said 'It is your love that I love most in this offering.'

kaiyil piṭicci ṭṭarutennu colliyō
rugminideviaṅgānoṭi
nārāyaṇā hare nārāyaṇā harē
ninneyariññavarāruṇḍu

Rukmini Devi pulled the bundle out of the Lords hands. She said 'enough' and ran away with the bundle of flattened rice. Victory to Narayana! What is there in this world that You do not know?

kaṇḍumaṭaṅgumbozhuḷḷam piṭakkyunni
tonnum parayāte pōnnitā

tāmarakkaṇṇane kaṇḍuḷḷanērattil
paṇḍuḷḷakālattil muṇgiyō

I am now on my way back, without having told Him anything of my sorrows. When I looked into His lotus eyes, did I become a child once more?

jīvitadukhaṅgaḷ onnum paraññilla
tannemarannatu tanneyā
nārāyaṇā harē nārāyaṇā harē
nīyariyāttat-entuṇḍu

I did not tell Him anything of my sorrows as I stood there forgetting myself, wrapped up in His love. Victory to Narayana! What is there in this world that You do not know?

Tāttinantam teytārā (Malayalam)

tāttinantam teytārā takatinantinam teytārā
tāttinantinam takatinantinam takatinantinam
teytārā
tāttinantinam takatinantinam takatinantinam
teytārā

pārvatinandanane karirūpamiyannavane
ādipūjita namaravandita
namṛtamānasanennayyan
kāttukoḷḷaṇam-iniyivanoru vazhiyaruḷaṇam-
enneykkum

O son of Parvati, You have the form of a black elephant. You are the god of new beginnings, adored by the immortal beings. Please protect me and forever guide me on my way.

nānmara nalporuḷē naṭamāṭum gaṇapatiyē
kāvyalōlupanamaranāṭaka
naṭanarasikanennayyan
kāttukoḷḷaṇam-iniyivanoru vazhiyaruḷēṇam-enneykkum

O Ganesh, the essence of the four Vedas. You relish dance, drama and poetry. O my Lord, please protect me and forever guide me on my way.

surajana vanditane munimānasa pūjitane
kāñcanaśobhita nadhikakōmaḷa natula
mohitanennayyan
kāttukoḷḷaṇam-iniyivanoru vazhiyaruḷēṇam-enneykkum

You are adored by the gods and worshipped by the sages. Your beautiful body shines like gold. O my Lord, please protect me and forever guide me on my way.

ṣaṇmukha-sōdarane siddhivināyakanē
nāradapūjita mānasavandita vighna-vināśakan-ennayyan
kāttukoḷḷaṇam-iniyivanoru vazhiyaruḷēṇam-enneykkum

Brother of Muruga, O Siddhi Vinayaka, You are worshipped by Sage Narada, and You are the remover of all obstacles. O my Lord, please protect me and forever guide me on my way.

śankaranandanane koṭum sankaṭanāśakanē
jñānadāyaka namalamānasa
nilayamarnnāṭumennayyan
kāttukoḷḷaṇam-iniyivanoru vazhiyaruḷēṇam-enneykkum

O Son of Shiva, You destroy extreme sorrow and bestow wisdom; You reside within a pure heart. O my Lord, please protect me and forever guide me on my way.

pāśānkuśadharane perumūṣika vāhananē
sūryasannidha nabhaya dāyakan-
ārttihārakanennayyan
kāttukoḷḷaṇam-iniyivanoru vazhiyaruḷēṇam-
enneykkum

You hold the rope and the elephant goad. You have the tiny mouse as Your vehicle and You shine like the sun. You protect us and destroy greed- O my Lord, please protect me and forever guide me on my way.

Tintinnam tintinnam (Malayalam)

tintinnam tintinnam takatimi tā
tintinnam tintinnam takatimi tā
takataka takataka takatimi tā
takataka takataka takatimi tā
takataka takataka takatimi tā

ceñcōra cempaṭṭu cilambaṇiyum
caṇḍikē pōrkkali kaḷiyāṭu nī
kaṭal pōle kaṭannēri kaḷiyāṭu nī
neṭumala tiṭam pōle naṭamāṭu nī
asurande gaḷamaruttaṭi vaykku nī

Wearing heavy anklets of red copper, O Chandika, You play the game of war. You wage war like the onrushing ocean. You danced as You slayed the demons.

teccippūmālayum aramaṇiyum
caṇḍikē pōrkkali kaḷiyāṭu nī
koṭunkāttu cuzhiyum pōl cuzhiññāṭu nī
kaṭutalaraṭikaḷāl naṭamāṭu nī
kaliyārnnu karaṅgaḷiṅgeṭuttāṭu nī

You wore tinkling hip chains and a red flower garland. O Chandika, You play the game of war. You play with Your enemies like a whirlwind that creates havoc. In your hands You angrily grab Your enemies and dance victoriously.

kolliyānoḷiyātta karavāḷavum
caṇḍikē pōrkkali kaḷiyāṭu nī
caṇḍamuṇḍa niṣudini naṭamāṭu nī
muṇḍamāla yulacculaccucculaññāṭu nī
mahiṣande śirassaruttaṭi vaykkū nī

You have lightning as Your bright sword, O Chandika, play the game of war! You destroyed the demons Chanda and Munda. Dance with the garland of skulls hanging around Your neck, You have manifested to destroy the demon Mahishasura.

kaṇkaḷil kaliyērum kanaloḷiyum
caṇḍikē pōrkkali kaḷiyāṭu nī
manassinde pōrkkaḷattilaṭi vaykku nī
duritaṅgaḷarutteriññuzhiññāṭu nī
uyirēkiyulakatte yuyarttīṭu nī

Your eyes burn like blazing coals. O Chandika, play the game of war! Please dance within the battle field of my heart! Cut away the miseries of my life. Grant a fresh new life and uplift the world.

Tum ho māte (Hindi)

tum ho māte varadā laḷite
dīnoddhāriṇi devī
karuṇādhārā ban śailsute
de sāre var jaldī

O Mother Lalita, You are the giver of boons and You uplift the sorrowful. Daughter of the mountain, river of compassion, please grant us all boons without delay!

jay jay mā jay jay mā
jay jay jay jay mā
jay mā mā mā mā
jay mā mā jay jay jay mā

Victory to Mother!

ham hai tere śaraṇāgat mā
tere āge-śīś-jhukātte
abhay de – māte
śaraṇ de – māte
tum hame – māte
nirupam sukh de tumī bacāvo

Mother we are surrendered to You, we bow our heads before You. Please reside in our hearts always. Mother, please protect us by bestowing incomparable happiness on us!

girije gaurī gatidāyini tū
sabko mangaḷ denā mā
abhay de – māte
śaraṇ de – māte
tum hame – māte
caraṇ kamal me sadā basāvo

O Daughter of the Mountain, Parvati, You are the giver of higher births. Mother, please bestow auspiciousness to all of us. O Mother, please promise to protect us and grant us refuge, please grant us shelter at Your lotus feet forever.

Undan tōḷil (Tamil)

undan tōḷil nānum sāyndu tūnkavēṇḍumē
undan anbukkāga maṭṭum ēnka vēṇḍumē
pārppatellām nīyenṭruṇarum pānku vēṇḍumē
bhavatāriṇi un tiruvaṭi tale tānka vēṇḍumē

Mother, I want to sleep on Your shoulder. I want to yearn only for Your love. I want the understanding that everything I see is You. You are the One who takes us across the ocean of samsara. I want to hold Your lotus feet on my head.

unnai tēṭi nāṭum nalla uḷḷattinaippeṭrēn
ennai nāṭi nīyum tēṭum pēṭṭrinaippeṭṭrēn
unnai tēṭi amaidi koḷḷum manadinaippeṭṭrēn
ennai tēṭi ammā nīyum enna tānpeṭṭrāy
ennai tān peṭṭrāy

I have the inclination to search for You and know You. I have received the blessing that You Yourself searched and found me. What did You gain, Mother, by searching for me?

enkē nānum irundapōdum ennai pārkkinṭrāy
edanai nānum pēsinālum nīyum kēṭkinṭrāy
tankum namadu uravu enṭru tāyum solkinṭrāy
tazhaikkum undan vāzhvu enṭru dayavum seykinṭrāy
dayavum seykinṭrāy

Wherever I am, You see me. Whatever I say, You listen to me. You affirm that our relationship will last forever. You shower Your compassion for my life to become fruitful.

Vandē vēdamayīm (Sanskrit)

vande vedamayīm vande devamayīm
vande śāstramayīm vande stotramayīm
vande amṛtamayīm vande yogamayīm
vande prāṇamayīm vande pūrṇamayīm

I praise the One who embodies knowledge, divinity, scriptures and praises, immortal nectar, divine union, life force and fullness.

bhāratabhuvamāgatya narāṇām hitam-
udbodhayasi
tvam hitamudbodhayasi
mānava-sevanatyāgakarmaṇā racayasi
navacaritam
iha janayasi navakiraṇam
tvam asmākam dharmarūpiṇi poṣaṇakartri sadā
jagadāśrayadātrī sadā
praṇamati tava śatakōṭi sutāvaliranupama
padakamalam
tava nirmalacaraṇayugam

Having come to this land of Bharat, You awaken the good in human beings. Through service to mankind and a life of sacrifice, You create a new history; You produce new rays of light here. You are our form of dharma, always the giver of refuge, always the giver of nourishment. Your hundred crore sons and daughters bow to Your lotus feet, Your pure feet.

karuṇāpūrṇaiḥ smitavacanaistvam
āmayamapanayasi
mama āmayamapanayasi
duḥkhita-dīnajanān-uddhartum jīvanamarpayasi
tvam jīvanamarpayasi
mañjuḷahāsini karmavilāsini hṛdi mama-
nivasasadā
tvam parilasa manasi sadā
ānandāmṛta-sneham pūraya pālayamām aniśam
bhuvi poṣayamām aniśam

With the fullness of Your compassion and Your smiling words, my confusion is removed. You have offered Your life for the sake of uplifting sad and helpless people. You have a beautiful smile and You work charmingly. Please reside in my heart and appear in my mind always. Shower Your joyful, immortal love, and guard me day and night, nourish me day and night...

Vicalita vāgade (Kannada)

vicalita vāgade irali ī manavu
nina caraṇa dhyānadindinitu
hariyali mananadi ninneḍege satata
acalavāgali ī manavu

Do not let my mind swerve even a little from this one-pointed meditation on Your feet. May the river of my mind flow endlessly in Your direction. May this mind become still.

cañcala cittake prapañca nīḍide
miñci miruguva māyālōka
kāmakrōdhada kēkekēḷiyō!
madamātsarya aṭṭahāsavō!

kūtalu konkadirali initu
ninadū... ī manavu

The wavering mind finds in the world of illusion a world of glitter: the laughter of lust and anger. Delirious laughter of pride and jealousy... May I not be disturbed, may not even a single hair become affected. This mind belongs to You.

cañcala cittake manadalē sikkidē
ēri iḷiyuva bhrāntibhramē
duḥkha duguḍada cakravyūhavō!
vyathe vāsanē ālasyavō!
kūdalu konkadirali initu
ninadū... ī manavu

This wavering mind finds itself within. The rise and fall of illusion and delusion, the vicious circle of sorrow and fear; suffering, vasanas (latent tendencies) and lethargy. May I not be disturbed, may not even a single hair become affected. My mind belongs to You.

Viṭhal smaraṇ karā

śrutvā viṭhalasya abhangam mānasam prasannam
hari darśanenāpi, mānasam prasannam

Hearing the praises of Lord Vitthala, and beholding the vision of Lord Hari, the mind becomes content.

viṭhal smaraṇ karā
viṭhal bhajan karā
viṭhobhāce dhyān karā
hṛday premāne bharā

Remember Vithala, sing the glory of Vithala! Remember and chant the holy name of Sri Hari.

vāṭ pāhū mī kitī varṣāne
mantr japū mī aho din rātrī
taṭpat āhe jīv hā māzā
ās lāgalī tujhyā darśanācī

After many thousands of years, You attained this human birth. There is no guarantee that this fortune will come back again; therefore, always seek the lotus feet of Vithala. Accomplish the very purpose of life by chanting His name.

jayahari viṭhala pāṇḍuranga jayaśrīranga pāṇḍuranga
paṇḍarīnātha pāṇḍuranga pāhipāhimām pāṇḍuranga

O Vithala, Panduranga, victory to You! O Lord of Pandari, please protect us!

samsārācī nāhī icchā
caraṇ vandan hīc apekṣā
yeśīl kadī tū paṇḍarīnāthā
sāyujy sukh de rakhumāyīnāthā

Wake up, wake up man! Proceed along the path of devotion. If you are lucky you could be blessed with the company of virtuous men; take this opportunity to sing the glory of Pandarinatha. Benefit from the grace of the real Sadguru!

jayahari viṭhala pāṇḍuranga
jayaśrīranga pāṇḍuranga
viṭhala viṭhala viṭhala viṭhala...

Yād rakh bande (Hindi)

yād rakh bande mere
jag musāfir khāna
kuch dino ke mehamān ham
ek din hai jānā

Remember friend, this world is but a traveller's rest house. For a few days only we are guests here, one day we will have to leave.

saje ḍhaje kāye ko
miṭṭi me mil jānā
miṭṭi me mil jānā
tan man dhan sab
choḍ ke hai jānā
choḍ ke hai jānā

One day this well-decorated body will inevitably meet dust; body, mind, and wealth will have to leave one day.

sage sambandhi tere
kām na ānā koyi
kām na ānā
citā jale...
citā jalte hī unko
vāppas hai jānā – ghar
vāppas hai jānā

All your close relatives will be of no use to you when your pyre burns... And no sooner than your pyre is burnt they will have to return to their homes.

jīna uskā jīna hai jo
satko pehacāna
satko pehacāna
maraṇ ke ānepar...
āttā hai hasna - use
āttā hai hasna

The one who truly lives is the one who recognizes the Truth. The one who knows to smile upon the arrival of death.

Yād teri vic (Punjabi)

yād teri vic dil par āyā
hañcu ḍul ḍul nirantar pende
agan birhādi lāge dil vicc
daras nīr barsā de
daras nīr barsā de

Remembering You, my tears flow unceasingly. The fire of separation burns in me. Do cool me with Your vision...

o maiyyā merī maiyyā
o maiyyā pyārī maiyyā

O my Mother, my darling Mother!

e sūraj prakāś tere nū
hāl merā suṇā de
lāl terā rāh takdā teri
dhaḍkan rukdi jāve
dhaḍkan rukdi jāve

O Sun, through your rays please convey my plight: 'Your darling child is pining for You. Even the next heartbeat seems unbearable.'

jīvan de har rang de utte
rang terā he caṭayā
bin tere har pal iñc lāge
jugjug bīte jāvaṇ
jugjug bīte jāvaṇ

In every color of life I have only found the color of You. Without You, each moment is agony and endless like many lifetimes.

murjhā rahā hai phullo terā
khuśbu uṭdi jāve
der na kari o maiyyā meri
pattiyā chaṭdi jāvaṇ
pattiyā chaṭdi jāvaṇ

All the flowers are wilting, their fragrance is fading, the leaves are all shedding away. Do not delay, O Mother!

Yaśodānā lāl (Gujarati)

yaśodānā lāl nāgar nandnā kumār prabhu
ṭhumak ṭhumak cāl sāthe cālyā kyā
ṭhumak ṭhumak cāl sāthe cālyā kyā

O Krishna, darling son of Yashoda and Nanda, walking with an attractive gait, where are You going?

māthe mor pankh dhari pīḷā pītāmbar ōḍhi
matvāli cāl sāthe cālyā kyā
koyinī maṭkī phoḍi koyinā mākhaṇcoryā
dekhi yaśodāne doḍi gayā kyā
dekhi yaśodāne doḍi gayā kyā

Dressed in yellow robes, a peacock feather tucked in Your hair, where are You going, Krishna? You break the pots of some gopis, steal their butter, and at the sight of Yashoda, where are You running to hide?

bhaktonā dilmā vase ānkhothi ojhal rahe
śodhe yaśodā dekhāy nahi
triloknā nāth prabhu em kem āvehāth
premthi pokāro doḍi āve kān
premthi pokāro doḍi āve kān

He dwells in the hearts of His devotees and remains invisible to the gross eye. Yashoda is looking for Him everywhere, but in vain. How can one catch the Lord of the three worlds? Call Him with love, and Krishna will come running.

premthi pokāro kān
premthi pokāro nām

Call Krishna with love, call His name with love.

yaśodānā lālni - jay kanaiyā lālki
bālgopālni - jay kanaiyā lālki
he līlādhāmni - jay kanaiyā lālki

Victory to Yashoda's son, victory to baby Krishna, victory to the player of divine plays.

www.ingramcontent.com/pod-product-compliance
Lightning Source LLC
Chambersburg PA
CBHW070621050426
42450CB00011B/3096